I DON'T NEED THIS STUFF!

Or Do I?

I DON'T NEED THIS STUFF!

Or Do I?

A Study Skills and Time Management Book

Stephen Piscitelli

Florida Community College at Jacksonville

HARCOURT BRACE COLLEGE PUBLISHERS

Fort Worth   Philadelphia   San Diego   New York   Orlando   Austin   San Antonio
Toronto   Montreal   London   Sydney   Tokyo

Publisher	•	Christopher P. Klein
Senior Acquisitions Editor	•	Carol Wada
Developmental Editor	•	Scott Stephens
Project Editor	•	Kylie E. Johnston
Production Manager	•	Eddie Dawson
Senior Art Director	•	Don Fujimoto

ISBN: 0-15-504059-6

Library of Congress Catalog Card Number: 96-77281

Copyright © 1997 by Harcourt Brace & Company

Address for Editorial Correspondence:
Harcourt Brace College Publishers, 301 Commerce Street, Suite 3700, Fort Worth, TX 76102.

Address for Orders:
Harcourt Brace & Company, 6277 Sea Harbor Drive, Orlando, FL 32887-6777. 1-800-782-4479,
or 1-800-433-0001 (in Florida).

Harcourt Brace College Publishers may provide complimentary instructional aids and supplements or supplement packages to those adopters qualified under our adoption policy. Please contact your sales representative for more information. If as an adopter or potential user you receive supplements you do not need, please return them to your sales representative or send them to:

Attn: Returns Department
Troy Warehouse
465 South Lincoln Drive
Troy, MO 63379

"Theories of Stratification" from SOCIOLOGY IN A CHANGING WORLD, Third Edition by William Komblum, copyright © 1994 by Holt, Rinehart and Winston, Inc. pages 373-376, reprinted by permission of the publisher.

Excerpts from CONTEMPORARY BUSINESS, Eighth Edition by Louis E. Boone and David L. Kurtz, copyright © 1996 by The Dryden Press, pp. 122-130, reprinted by permission of the publisher.

Jeanne Sadler, "Home Economics 101," *The Wall Street Journal,* October 14, 1994, p. R12. Reprinted by permission of *The Wall Street Journal,* © 1994 Dow Jones & Company, Inc. All Rights Reserved Worldwide.

Printed in the United States of America

6 7 8 9 0 1 2 3 4 5   066   10 9 8 7 6 5 4 3 2 1

To all of my students—
past, present, and future.

You are the reason
I teach.
You are my
motivation to focus
on success.

Preface

This book focuses on student behavior. I have written this book visualizing how a student sitting across the table from me would discuss and use the material presented. The numerous self-assessment tools throughout the text will engage students in customizing and using the book's advice. This book will help them change their actions and behavior to become more successful.

This emphasis on assessment and application does not mean that theory is unimportant. Educational theory underscores many of the concepts presented in the following pages. Sometimes, however, books can get bogged down in jargon. A student struggling to do well in a course needs practical strategies and tips based on theory in order to succeed. This book provides that.

OVERVIEW OF THE CHAPTERS

I Don't Need This Stuff! Or Do I? gives students information, strategies, and tips in all areas of study skills.

Introduction
This chapter introduces the student to the philosophy of the book. This is not a beat-the-system approach. Being a successful student requires work and individual responsibility.

The student is also introduced to the concept of learning styles. An informal learning style assessment inventory is presented. This information will be utilized throughout the book. Each chapter ends with suggested ways to correlate students' learning style to some of the strategies presented in the preceding pages.

I Want To Run My Own Life
Students need to know the characteristics of a successful student as well as where their own strengths and weaknesses lie. Activities include an analysis of study skill scenarios and an assessment of the student's academic and organizational skills.

This inventory is a logical departure point for the next topic—goal setting. Activities guide the student through the process of establishing meaningful and realistic goals. The student is shown, step-by-step, how to establish long-range, mid-range, and short-range academic and life goals.

So Many Assignments—So Little Time
Now that a goal has given the student purpose, it's time to organize for action. Some activities in this chapter help students find out what causes time management problems in their life and how to remedy those problems. Other activities help them break down large projects into more manageable steps.

Finally, students not only learn the art of prioritizing tasks, but also how to maintain a balance in life. Urgency, importance, effectiveness, and efficiency are put in a realistic context.

The Classroom Experience

Each instructor has a unique style of delivery and a particular emphasis in class. This chapter helps students be successful by understanding these styles and working with them. Common distractions are explained along with strategies to combat them.

In addition to looking at the teacher's job of teaching, students learn their jobs. Active learning, note-taking strategies, and effective review techniques are introduced. Students can practice various strategies to organize and reorganize material so that they can understand the big picture as well as the supporting details.

I Have to Read 1,000 Pages by When?

This chapter helps students prepare for and read a textbook efficiently and effectively. To understand a reading assignment, students must first approach it in an organized fashion. They must orient themselves to the subject matter and anticipate what may be covered. Then they need to implement an effective reading plan. This chapter gives students strategies to successfully complete assigned readings.

That Sounds Good—But I Have No Idea What It Means

This section of the text is a simple approach to get the student writing and remain focused until the final product is completed. The T.O.E.S. method of organization—Topic, Opinion, Evidence, and Summary—is introduced. A 10-point checklist is provided so students can complete their own evaluation of a writing project.

Once students know how to organize their ideas and write a paper, they're ready to do research in the library. I go over what students will need to know to start doing research and where to look for information. A general overview of narrowing a topic, managing time, and negotiating through the library is presented.

Whatshisname Scheduled a Whatchamacallit for When?

A key to a more effective memory is the ability to concentrate. The first part of this chapter discusses the causes for retrieval failure as well as strategies to improve retention and recall. Active listening, data retrieval, chart development, peg systems, acronyms, and acrostics are some of the techniques introduced. The entire chapter reinforces the need to establish relationships, which ties in with strategies introduced in previous topics.

There's No Business Like Prep Business—
The Art of Being Ready When Duty Calls

This chapter on test anxiety helps students recognize the causes of test anxiety and how to overcome its effects. The strategies in this chapter not only build on the previous seven topics, but they also set the stage for more goal-setting. The test preparation checklist guides the student through steps from studying for a test to post-exam analysis. Although it is not recommended, tips are provided for "emergency studying."

Some Final Comments

In this chapter I help the student put the whole book in perspective and remember the important points. The P.O.P. R.A.P. list summarizes these main principles.

The strategies and tips presented in the book help students at any stage in their college career. Some will even help them with life in general! Because of the quantity and diversity of strategies in this book, students are encouraged to pick and choose the techniques that fit their personality and work for them. These strategies have helped students minimize failures and maximize successes.

Acknowledgments

Writing a book requires some knowledge, a good deal of persistence, and a great amount of ego, especially for a how-to book like this. After all, I am presenting what I think to be the most effective ways to do something. Ego is a necessary fuel in this production process.

But as with anything, if a proper balance is not maintained, the book can easily lose focus and stray from its original purpose. That is where the following people helped. I asked them to review, correct, suggest, redline, praise, and otherwise provide honest feedback. After months of writing, the author is too close to the project to realistically appraise its worth. So, before you read the following pages I want to give credit to those folks who had the laborious and tedious task of helping me organize and express my thoughts.

- Elizabeth Renfroe for the mechanical review. She had the task of keeping my thoughts parallel and my infinitives in their proper place.

- Rebecca Reichenberg for both the perspective of a parent and a returning adult college student. She has been very active in her boys' education and knows, firsthand, the challenges both students and parents face.

- Stephanie Shackelford for the ability to detect fluff and garbage. As the parent of a teenage daughter, Stephanie knows the difference between practical strategies and educational drivel.

- Nancy Woodward for the classroom perspective. Nancy is a recognized master teacher. For more than two decades she has worked with middle school students. She knows the unique challenges that middle school students, parents, and teachers face daily.

- Jim November for the encouragement. Jim was available during those times of confusion when a little "truing" of the course was necessary. His advice helped me focus on my end result.

- The staff of Hope Haven Children's Clinic and Family Center in Jacksonville, Florida, for their support and encouragement. Hope Haven has been the site of many of my study skills seminars.

- All of my former students who have taught me as much as I have taught them. Schools, teachers, seminars, and the like can only exist because of students. The students are the customers we must serve. This book is very much a product of our interactions.

- My colleagues at college campuses across the country, particularly J. Darlene Thomas and Dee Bostick at Midlands Technical College; Tamara Brawner at Thomas College; Mary Bixby at University of Missouri at Columbia; Mary Wolting at Indiana University—Purdue University at Indianapolis; Dennis Nelson at Willmar Community College; and Lucy Tribble MacDonald at Chemeketa Community College.

- The editorial and production staff at Harcourt Brace who were key in getting my ideas into this book and out to you. Carol Wada first expressed interest in the book and guided it through publication. Her faith, guidance, and encouragement during the project are the reasons the manuscript was accepted and the book published. Kylie Johnston, Eddie Dawson, and Don Fujimoto did a remarkable job with design and production of the book. And, of course I thank my friend Nick Speckman whose interest in this book was very instrumental in getting it published at Harcourt Brace.

- My wife, Laurie, for the countless hours of listening, critiquing and prodding. Laurie has not only read manuscript drafts, but she has constantly challenged me to use my talents to enhance my students' performance. Her hours are too numerous to count; her love an inspiration. My gratitude can never be appropriately expressed.

All of us—the individuals listed above and myself—wish you success on your journey to become a more successful student.

Contents

About the Author

Stephen Piscitelli earned his undergraduate degree from Jacksonville University, his M.Ed. from the University of North Florida, and his M.A. in history from the University of Florida.

Stephen has been a classroom instructor since 1982, teaching middle school to college level students of varying abilities. He has been an instructor at the community college level since 1988, and in 1993 he established an educational consulting firm, which develops and delivers training seminars to students as well as teachers.

Stephen lives with his wife Laurie and two canine companions in Jacksonville, Florida.

CHAPTER 1

INTRODUCTION

✔ **Introduction**
- **Goals**
- **Time management**
- **Classroom expectations**
- **Reading strategies**
- **Writing and research strategies**
- **Memory and relationships**
- **Test preparation**
- **Summary**

1. **What is this book all about, anyway?**
   What this book will *not* do for you
   What this book *will* do for you
2. **Learning styles**
   One size does not fit all
   How do *you* learn?
   What does all this mean to me?
3. **A quick review**

Far better it is to dare mighty things,
to win glorious triumphs, even though checkered
with failure, than to take rank with those poor
spirits who neither enjoy much nor suffer much,
because they live in the grey twilight that
knows not victory nor defeat.

—Theodore Roosevelt

WHAT IS THIS BOOK ALL ABOUT, ANYWAY?

Some helpful sources on the market today address the topics I do. I have listed these folks in the bibliography. But I believe this book goes further. For instance:

(1) **The topic is serious; the tone is light. You won't get lost in research jargon or confusing graphics;**
(2) **The techniques have been developed and used in public-school classrooms and private seminars;**
(3) **The tips and strategies have been refined at the college level;**
(4) **Parents, as well as classroom teachers, have reviewed the content and suggested improvements that have been incorporated throughout the chapters; and**
(5) **This material is fresh. Students are currently using these tips.**

What this book will not *do for you*

Many books offer ways to beat the system in order to earn the highest possible grade. That is like going on a fad diet to lose weight but never changing the behaviors that resulted in the undesired extra baggage. If it were as simple as just reading a book or watching a video, you, your classmates, and most other students would be happy with your high GPAs. Unfortunately, it is not that easy.

If you want a quick-fix approach offering instant gratification, this is not the book. There is nothing wrong with going for the best grade, but you must focus on your behaviors. And that's what this book does.

What this book will *do for you*

It will help you identify and change those behaviors that are keeping you from being the very best student you can be. Its overriding purpose is to help you focus on your strengths while working to reduce your weaknesses. The central concept is organization. I will show you that good study habits do not necessarily mean an increased work load. Efficient studying enables you to study more effectively.

This book is more than enrichment—and it most definitely is *not* remediation. It concentrates on practical skills to build academic success as well as a positive self-image.

While it is worthwhile for students at every level, it is particularly valuable to those individuals who have the potential and desire, in an increasingly competitive academic world, to obtain the "added edge" needed for academic success. These are the skills needed to make the transition from a student who simply gets by to a successful student who is shrewd, insightful, and confident.

In order to achieve at above-average academic levels, you need to develop techniques to focus your energies on efficient and effective studying. Additionally, the acquisition and implementation of proficient study skills is crucial in the development of positive self-esteem. A student who can achieve in the classroom will feel better about his or her capabilities. In other words, **<u>competence</u> will foster <u>esteem.</u>**

Specifically, if you diligently follow the suggestions in this book you will learn:

more than 200 tips, strategies, and activities to help you become a more effective and efficient student. Once I present these techniques, my job is complete—and yours is just beginning. You will need to commit to three very simple tasks: <u>learn</u> the strategies; <u>use</u> the strategies immediately; and continually <u>practice</u> the strategies.

one size does not fit all. Each of us has a unique learning style. Identify it; make adjustments and see the success.

the motivation to do well is within you. External influences may cause a temporary burst of inspiration. For the long term, however, you must have confidence in your abilities, address your shortcomings, and develop an internal gyroscope that will guide you through school—and through life.

all of the strategies come down to organization. Successful students have it; those without it struggle.

the strategies contained in this book are also excellent life-management tools. These techniques are easily transferable to everyday life.

This book is the result of ongoing experience with students. These techniques work. Learn them, apply them, and practice them.

You can become a successful student.

LEARNING STYLES

One size does not fit all

Imagine this. You walk into a doctor's office and announce, "Doc, I'm out of sorts. Fix me." Any reasonable doctor would first need to know some specifics: What are your symptoms? What medications are you currently taking? To what drugs are you allergic?

In other words, the doctor has to recognize you as an individual patient with distinct and separate characteristics from other clients in the waiting room.

The same goes for study skills. You are a unique student. A prescribed study skill for a classmate might not be appropriate for you.

You will be given many suggestions in the next several chapters. You need to pick and choose those which best fit your learning style. (This isn't permission to reject those strategies which seem to be too much work. Many will require some additional effort at first.) Be mindful of how you learn. You should be aware of the conditions which work best for you: absolute quiet or background noise? structure or flexibility? solitude or group interaction?

A word of warning: just because you do something now when you study, *does not* mean it is your learning style. It might be your *preference,* but that does not mean it is how you *learn.* If we are honest with ourselves, we will probably find that a lot of habits are not productive to task accomplishment. I've heard students proudly state, "I can study while watching the football game." In reality, they are going through the motions of studying. The quality of learning taking place under these conditions is questionable at best.

How do *you* learn?

Very simply, "learning style" refers to the manner in which individuals process information.[1] This book does not attempt to be the definitive source on learning styles. My purpose is to raise your level of awareness about *your* style. I want you to become more in tune with the best way you learn. The material in this section just scratches the surface. In fact, a lot of work has been done recently in the area of multiple intelligences. This theory addresses "the broad range of abilities that humans possess by grouping their capabilities into seven comprehensive categories of intelligence."[2] Nothing so profound is attempted here.

Take a moment and complete the following inventory. Please keep in mind that this is not a scientific instrument. It is simply a method for you to become more sensitive to what works and does not work for you.

HOW DO I LEARN BEST?

Please circle the items that apply to you. When choosing, ask yourself if this is the manner that produces the best results *for you.*

When studying, I *most often* do best when . . .

1. the room is brightly lit
2. the room is lit by one light at my study area
3. the room is more cold than warm
4. the room is more warm than cold
5. I sit in a hard, straight-backed chair at a desk
6. I sit in a comfortable chair at a desk
7. I recline on the floor
8. I schedule a particular time for school work
9. I hear things rather than read things
10. I see things rather than hear them
11. someone explains a process to me

12. I can physically assemble something myself
13. I move around the room
14. I sit on the edge of my chair
15. I have just finished a meal
16. it is early in the day
17. it is late in the day
18. I work by myself
19. I work in groups
20. I take breaks
21. I sit for long periods of time, without a break, and completely finish a project
22. there are very few distractions
23. there is soft background noise
24. there is loud music
25. there is absolute quiet
26. I can draw illustrations to accompany the material I am learning
27. I can hold something (like a rubber ball, a small bean bag) while studying
28. I can do an experiment rather than write a paper
29. my parents, friends, or roommates ask me to explain a new concept I have learned
30. I quickly survey an assignment so that I can see what is coming
31. I am quizzed by a parent, friend, or roommate
32. I can watch a movie of a novel I have just read
33. there is an open window
34. I have no set study time
35. I read aloud when completing a reading assignment
36. I can associate a picture with the name of a personality or an event
37. I am free to motivate myself to complete my assignments
38. someone stays "on top of me" with deadlines and structure
39. I am allowed to be curious and explore without rigid guidelines
40. I know exactly what is expected
41. I can take risks
42. things are presented in an ordered or chronological fashion
43. List any other characteristics that apply to your learning style:

_____

_____

_____

_____

_____.

We are all affected differently by various factors from environment to manner of presentation by the teacher. Take a moment to group the items you circled above. You will most likely fall into one of three broad learning style categories:

auditory: learn by hearing
kinesthetic: learn by doing, touching, and moving
visual: learn by seeing

Additionally, you will notice there are a variety of environmental factors that may alter your productivity:[3]

food and drink
light
sound
temperature
comfort of furniture
structure of time and/or task
ability to move about
peer interaction

What conclusions can you draw about your style? Write a brief description of the manner in which you learn. How do you know this is accurate? List specific examples from your academic experience to support your conclusion.

_____

_____

_____

_____

_____

_____

_____

What does all this mean to me?

The intent is not to give you a rigid label. There will be times when you learn very well by visual means and times when auditory techniques are more productive. Individual work might be your normal routine, but a study group can be appropriate when trying to understand a troubling concept. The point is to understand what works best *most of the time.*

STRATEGY #1   As you proceed through this book, keep your learning style in mind. For instance, a "visual" student might have more success with the Cluster Note format found on page 56 than the traditional outline on page 55. Although this will be called to your attention in each chapter, your first assignment is to be vigilant as you read. What strategies fit *your* style of processing information? This will engage you as an active, rather than a passive, learner. More importantly, it puts *you* in control of your academic process and progress.

Understanding your learning styles is one more weapon in your arsenal against poor school performance. Use the knowledge productively.[4]

A QUICK REVIEW

The topic of study skills involves more than spending hours staring into a pile of books and homework assignments. It does concern:

- efficient and effective studying;
- practical skills combined with potential and desire;
- competence combined with responsibility;
- practicing new strategies;
- organization;
- picking strategies which fit your own learning style; and
- putting you in control of your academic progress.

CHAPTER 2

I WANT TO RUN MY OWN LIFE

- • Introduction
- ✔ **Goals**
- • Time management
- • Classroom expectations
- • Reading strategies
- • Writing and research strategies
- • Memory and relationships
- • Test preparation
- • Summary

1. What are study skills—and why do I need them?
What does a successful student look like?
What you need to do
A word about self-esteem
What do you think of when you hear the term "study skills"?
If completing an assignment is not studying—what is?
I want to learn—but I can't!

2. Motivational goal setting
If you want someone else to run your life, skip this section and move
to Chapter 3
I don't have time for this stuff
"Meaningful specific" or "Wandering generality"
What does a clearly stated goal look like?
W.I.N.
Evaluate your goals: Wanting to do something is not the same thing as
doing something

3. A quick review

> *Destiny is no matter of chance.*
> *It is a matter of choice.*
> *It is not a thing to be waited for,*
> *it is a thing to be achieved.*
>
> —*William Jennings Bryan*

WHAT ARE STUDY SKILLS—AND WHY DO I NEED THEM?

Let's face it—given a choice of activities, reading a study skills book would probably not be a popular selection for most people. But you have chosen to read this—and that gives you a tremendous head start over someone with less motivation. You are about to embark on a journey—a journey that, quite frankly, is not for everyone. This book is for individuals interested in becoming *successful students*.

What does a successful student look like?

Read each of the following scenarios. After each description do the following: (1) Write whether or not you think the student is using effective study strategies; and (2) Identify what is "good" and what the student could do better.

A. Mike had quite a lot of homework for the evening. "I hate this stuff," he said. "It's so boring, boring, boring!" After ten minutes of griping, he sat on his bed, looked at the stack of books in front of him, and pulled out the closest one. It happened to be his history book. "Yuck! Who cares about what happened 300 years ago?" He turned to chapter 14 and immediately started reading. A few minutes later he switched on his radio for some background noise. Back to his book he went. The phone rang. He jumped to answer it. "Anything's better than this stuff," he groaned. Twenty-five minutes later he finished talking. Back to the history book. He flipped through the rest of the pages, looked at some of the pictures, and said, "Mr. P. will never ask me a question anyway." He then went to his math homework. This course was giving him the most problems this year. "I need to be comfortable for this." He grabbed his pillow, got on his stomach and started flipping through the problems. He couldn't remember how the teacher had done the problems today. He had copied similar problems from the board in class, but those were back at school in his notebook—which was in his locker. "Oh, well. I'll get the answers tomorrow from Steve." It was now about fifteen minutes before Monday Night Football. He quickly looked at the science book. "Good," he thought, "only five pages to read." With one eye on the clock and one on the book, he quickly scanned the reading. "No problem. The test isn't until next week." At 9:00 p.m. he slammed the book closed. "I've been studying for three hours! What else can they expect from me? Time for a break."

Please write your evaluation of Mike's study skills:

_____

_____

_____

_____

B. Bubba had about two hours of homework ahead of him tonight. He went to the kitchen table, took out his assignment pad, and reviewed his assignments for the evening. "It looks like math will take me about forty-five minutes, history reading about thirty, the English grammar exercise should only be about fifteen minutes, and Spanish vocabulary—well, that's my toughest and it'll take a good thirty minutes to review." Although he wasn't excited about it, he pulled out his Spanish flash cards and began reviewing. "Might as well get this out of the way first," he said. Thirty minutes later he took a five-minute break to get a glass of water and to stretch. Back to work he went. He worked through his list taking breaks every twenty or thirty minutes. He finished his homework in time to play a computer game before going to bed.

Please write your evaluation of Bubba's study skills:

_____

_____

_____

_____

C. Lucy was having a tough year in school. It seemed she was always behind. And each course was a struggle. "I'm doing a total of one hour of homework every night, but my grades sure don't reflect it! And those teachers do nothing but assign one project after another. My science research experiment is just around the corner. Thank goodness my outline's not due for another month." Tonight was one of those rare nights—no assigned homework! Yeah! "I'm going to rest. I deserve it, and anyway there's no homework." With that she turned on the TV and called a friend.

Please write your evaluation of Lucy's study skills:

_____

_____

_____

_____

❖❖❖

Who has the characteristics of a successful student? Who seems to have an effective approach to the tasks at hand? Who has the winning attitude? (That *is* vital.) You may have identified some of the following study skills (and lack thereof):

Mike:

Poor attitude. "I hate this stuff . . . Yuck! . . .What else can they expect from me?"

Study space. Given the little we know of Mike, it is questionable whether his bed is the best location to study. It may be too comfortable.

Purpose in reading? He immediately starting reading his assignment. No warm-up, no skimming, no orientation as to what was important.

Distractions. The radio and the telephone don't seem to be ingredients of an effective study equation.

Lack of focus. He "flipped through" his pages "with one eye on the clock." Mike is not giving full attention to his work.

Timing. Math is his most difficult course, yet he does not tackle it first when his energy level is (or should be) at its highest.

Academic tools. Why is his math notebook not at home with him?

Realistic assessment. Mike might have opened his books three hours ago, but he certainly has not been studying for three hours. He is deluding himself.

Bubba:

Assignment pad. Bubba has a written log of his homework. He can work from this to organize his studies for the evening.

Organized. He takes a moment to map out the study schedule for the evening.

Priorities. Bubba knows what causes him the most difficulties. He is going to focus his energies on this while he is the freshest.

Flash cards. He has found a technique that helps him effectively store information.

Breaks. He knows the power of taking a short time-out to refresh his attention.

Reward. When Bubba completes his work, he takes time for himself to do something totally unrelated to academics. Not only is he signaling an end to the day's studies, he is also providing balance for his life.

Lucy:

Always behind. The question for Lucy is "Why?" Are you giving enough effort? Do you stay current with reading and class work? Are you overplaced—in other words, are you in the right class?

One hour of homework. By time one gets to college, one hour of homework is definitely not a burden.

Attitude. Stop blaming the instructors. Accept responsibility.

No assigned homework. Really, now! Has she reviewed her notes from the day? Does she *have* any notes from the day? What about future projects? Any steps to be taken now? And if she is always behind, might this not be a great night to try to catch up?

Procrastination. The science project is due in a month. Why not accomplish a small step toward its completion?

Attitude, again. "I'm going to rest. I deserve it . . . ." Lucy sounds as if she has been doing quite a bit of resting!

What you need to do

Successful students are not necessarily the students who study the most or who have the highest IQs.

Read that sentence again. I want you to understand that the so-called smart students are really successful students who have mastered the art of ***focusing.*** These students have learned how to accomplish quality school work in shorter periods of time—leaving time for personal, non-academic goals.

More specifically, successful students are those students who:

- Focus on the *connection* between strengths and challenges. Too many times we look only at our weaknesses. Why not look at our strengths and use them to overcome our challenges? Always give yourself a pat on the back for what you do well. You can turn weaknesses into additional strengths.

- Focus on *desire*. You are the one responsible for good grades. Yes, you have teachers, but you have to have the will to be successful. Without this drive and motivation, you might as well put this book down now and turn on the television. As the Army says, "Be all you can be!"

- Focus on *responsibility*. You are responsible for yourself. Successful students know they need to *act on their environment,* rather than constantly reacting to *what happens to them.* You cannot control everything that comes your way—but with a little work, you will be able to minimize the times you cry out, "Why is this happening to me?"

- Focus on *attitude*. **Successful students *want* to be successful students!** Change the way you look at yourself. **Let's get rid of negative thoughts about ourselves.** This is a major premise of this book.

- Focus on *being an active learner*. Use as much of your brain as possible! One study skills expert[5] maintains that we use only three percent of our brains—only three percent! It has also been said that the brain is capable of handling about six-hundred words per minute; most people speak at about 125 words per minute.[6] What does that mean for the student in the classroom? Drifting attention may very well indicate you have a normally active brain—but remember our major purpose. You want to be successful, so you need to channel that activity in a positive manner.

- Focus on *achievement*—the added edge needed for academic excellence. There is competition in school. It is in the classroom, in the tryouts for the musical comedy or basketball team, and for admission to the school of your choice.

A word about self-esteem

What helps build positive self-esteem? Compliments are nice, but sometimes they are empty. If you turn in, for example, a poorly written essay and the teacher wants to "spare your feelings," he can write all sorts of nice comments on your paper (*"I like your penmanship"*). But this is useless for the successful student. You have received a compliment that has nothing to do with the task at hand. The skill has not been mastered.

 What is needed is confidence. Practicing a skill will develop a certain level of competence. Competence leads to confidence—and it is difficult for a confident individual to have poor self-esteem.

What do you think of when you hear the term "study skills"?

Most students approach a study skills course (or book) with less than a positive attitude. It's not one of the "most popular" topics in the course catalog. Typical responses include:

> Only dummies need this book.
> Why do I need this course? I do my homework every night. Isn't that studying?
> What makes smart students smart? How do they do it? They must do nothing but homework—bunch of nerds!
> My advisor made me take this course.
> My mother made me come to this course.

Interestingly enough, good grades do not have to be accompanied by hours of work. Please hear this: I have seen very capable students overdo it on homework. It is possible to overstudy, to stress, and to waste your energies. I'm not advocating that you stop working. But do it more efficiently. Here's an example.

Have you ever studied for a long time only to be baffled by a fat red "F" on an exam? Frustrating! I've heard many students complain, "I sat at that desk for hours last night—and I still bombed." Dr. Claude Olney made the point, in his program *Where There's a Will There's an A,* that given a list of tasks to remember, people will tend to remember best the first thing/group and the last thing/group of that list.[7]

The student who decides to study three hours, without a break, for an exam will more than likely remember what he studied at the very beginning and very end of the study time. Retention of the material in the middle is more questionable.

STRATEGY #2   Try, as Dr. Olney suggests, to break up your study period into, say, three one-hour blocks of time. Now, instead of just one start and one end point there are three starts and three ends. If his premise is correct, you are likely to remember six groups of items rather than just two.

STRATEGY #3   So, one of your first strategies is to give yourself a break when studying. Be reasonable and moderate in your approach. A related strategy is to give yourself an *appropriate* reward at each brief break. For instance, after one hour of reviewing your reading assignment, you can get a snack, or listen to five minutes of music, or just walk outside and play with the dog for a couple of minutes. The point is to stay fresh and alert. More is not necessarily better. Dr. Olney graphically shows the concept like this:

FIGURE 2.1

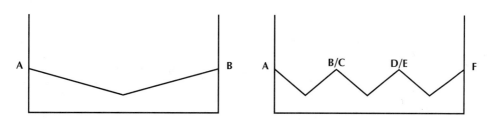

If you schedule breaks, homework will be less tedious. You will, also, have much more time left for studying.

"Wait a minute," you may say. "I thought I *was* just studying for three hours!" Well, maybe you were and maybe you weren't.

Smart students know that doing nightly homework is not necessarily studying. Doing your math problems, reading your history assignment, or completing a grammar exercise is not studying. Did you hear that? Read that sentence again.

If completing an assignment is not studying—what is?

The first time you are introduced to material, you are simply becoming familiar with the concepts. When you start reviewing and relating this material, *then* you are studying. You will learn more about this in later chapters. For the moment, understand that those successful students sitting next to you in class know *how* to study. It isn't magic—you can do it, too.

 You see, smart students know their challenges. They do not necessarily have high IQs. In fact, I've worked with a lot of high-IQ students who were *not* very smart. Smart means to be shrewd, which means to have keen insight. The point here is to know your strengths and weaknesses. Challenges may vary, but all of us must face them.

I want to learn—but I can't!

It is frustrating to have the desire but come up short on result. As you complete the following assessment, I want you to identify your obstacles to learning and your strengths that help you to process information. That is, what stands in your way of being as successful as you would like? Are the obstacles because of attitude? For instance, what is your attitude toward your own personal ability, your family's moral support, the process of learning, time management, and self-discipline? What helps you become a successful student?

Let's look at your Assessment of Strengths and Weaknesses. What are some of your academic challenges?

ASSESSMENT OF STRENGTHS AND WEAKNESSES

Before you can work on your challenges, you need to know what they are. That seems obvious, but sometimes we miss the obvious. So, take a moment right now and complete the following.

The challenges we want to concern ourselves with at this point are *process* challenges, not *content* challenges. You might be weak when it comes to solving geometric proofs, but I want you to concentrate on the *ways* in which you can become a more capable geometry student (or English, or history, or science, or Spanish . . .).

Circle your **strengths** when it comes to studying. What do you do well? Circle as many or as few as apply. Take your time and think about each choice carefully.

setting goals
completing goals
establishing priorities
completing work on time
eliminating distractions
taking notes from class lectures
taking notes from your textbook
taking organized notes
getting to class on time
participating in class
keeping an organized notebook
regularly reviewing class notes
getting the main point from a reading assignment
coming to class prepared
writing a strong thesis statement
being able to support an opinion with facts
organizing an essay
writing and completing an essay
establishing relationships
remembering important information for exams
controlling test anxiety
preparing, in plenty of time, for exams
completing exams in the time allotted
learning from previous exam mistakes
taking study breaks
studying alone
studying with friends

other:

_____

_____

_____

_____

Circle your **weaknesses** when it comes to studying. What do you need to improve? Circle as many or as few as apply. Take your time and think about each choice carefully.

setting goals
completing goals
establishing priorities
completing work on time
eliminating distractions
taking notes from class lectures
taking notes from your textbook
taking organized notes
getting to class on time
participating in class
keeping an organized notebook
regularly reviewing class notes
getting the main point from a reading assignment
coming to class prepared
writing a strong thesis statement
being able to support an opinion with facts
organizing an essay
writing and completing an essay
establishing relationships
remembering important information for exams
controlling test anxiety
preparing, in plenty of time, for exams
completing exams in the time allotted
learning from previous exam mistakes
taking study breaks
studying alone
studying with friends

other:

_____

_____

_____

_____

Now, rank order the top five items you circled in each section above. Number your greatest strength 1, and rank the other four by 2, 3, 4, and 5. Do the same for your weaknesses.

Remember the major premise of the book: You want to be a successful student. Now what can **you** do about these challenges?

The skills and strategies to overcome your challenges go beyond the classroom. Think of something you want in your personal life (make a sports team, meet a new friend, go to a particular concert). How would you go about accomplishing the task?

MOTIVATIONAL GOAL SETTING

If you wanted to become a member of an athletic team, earn first chair in the school band, win the lead in this year's drama production, how would you go about it? That is, how would you achieve your desired end? If you want to be successful, you will establish your goal (get the lead part) and then identify the steps you need to address in order to obtain what you want (rehearse the script, attend auditions, project your voice, exude confidence).

If you want someone else to run your life, skip this section and move to Chapter 3

STRATEGY #4

When it comes to success in the classroom, the same process should be used. What, after all, is more motivating than establishing what you want to achieve—and then pursuing that dream? You have to visualize your success. The first step is to establish a clearly stated plan of what you want, when you want it, and how you are going to get it. Goals need to be personal—not someone else's idea of what you should accomplish.

I don't have time for this stuff

The first time we try a new activity it is awkward. With practice, the process becomes habit, a natural part of us. Once you learn the art of goal setting, you will be well on your way to being a smart student.

"Meaningful specific" or "Wandering generality"

Goals provide focused direction. One activity I have conducted with students vividly gets the point across. I play the part of a person who wishes to take a vacation. The problem is I have no idea where I want to go, how much I want to spend, how much I have to spend, or anything else necessary to reach a destination. The students quickly grow frustrated trying to get me to a suitable location.

The same is true of your personal goals. If you do not know where you are headed, it is very difficult to reach your destination.

Zig Ziglar, motivational speaker from Dallas, Texas, reminds his audience of the need to be directed by goals. Ziglar emphasizes that people without well-written and well-attended goals are lost souls. He urges every audience member to evaluate whether or not he or she is a "meaningful specific or a wandering generality." In other words, do you have direction or not?[8]

What does a clearly stated goal look like?[9]

A clear goal is written. Once in writing, it becomes an affirmation of intent. Put it where you will see it every day. You cannot—and do not want to—ignore this important challenge you have established. Some people find the process of actually "writing" a goal to be awkward and a waste of time. But this is a valuable exercise as you develop the habit of establishing long-range plans. So, sharpen that pencil and write!

STRATEGY #5

A clear goal must be specific. Exactly what do you wish to accomplish? Saying,

"I want to raise my English grade"

is admirable, but it is incomplete. By how much do you wish to raise it? By when? How will you know when you achieve the goal? In other words, be specific and make it measurable.

"I want to get a "B" in English by the end of the semester"

is a much clearer statement of your desire. There is no doubt as to what you wish to accomplish.

A clear goal has to be realistic. It should be challenging, yet attainable. The deadline also must be "doable." Saying you will raise your English grade from an "F" to an "A" by the end of the week is not realistic. Challenge, but do not discourage yourself. I have seen students try to turn around an abysmal term, only to become discouraged because they set their sights unrealistically high. The sky may indeed be the limit, but make sure you know exactly where your sky is. My sky (ability level) is different than yours. Set high goals—but make sure they are realistic.

A clear goal must have a road map. Know where you are going, how you are going to get there, and when you plan on arriving. Otherwise you are aimless, clueless, and wasting your time. Simplify the goal into manageable and bite-sized steps. You have a long-range goal; now you need some short- and mid-range steps to achieve this goal. Look at the following diagram. Visualize your goal at the top of the triangle. What steps will you take to get there? Take your time. This is an important step. You want to *motivate* not *overwhelm* yourself.

Climbing the Mountain of Success

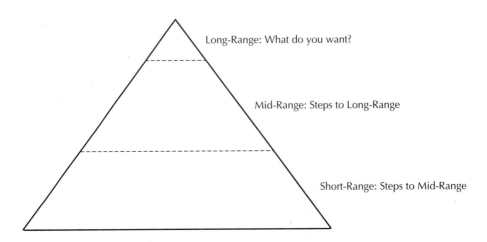

Long-Range: What do you want?

Mid-Range: Steps to Long-Range

Short-Range: Steps to Mid-Range

Here is an example of a road map:

Long-range:

To attain an A in math by the end of the semester

Mid-range:

1. Complete all assigned homework.
2. Correct and rework any problems marked incorrect on homework or tests.
3. See the instructor at least once a week for extra help. This may be for remediation or a chance to work additional problems.
4. Find a study group (if this fits your learning style).
5. Participate in class.
6. Get "As" on all the tests.

Short-range:

1. Get the class book(s).
2. Review the introduction and table of contents of the book(s).
3. Carefully read the instructor's course description, assignment page, and any other handout.

 A clear goal has anticipated the glitch factor. As Murphy has known for so long, if something can go wrong, it probably will. Your goals are not immune to this universal law. Don't become paranoid, but do try to anticipate some of the problems you may encounter along the way. If you do so, obstacles will not be a surprise—and they will not be so demoralizing.

A clear goal has built-in incentives. Even though you want to reach a point where your goals are intrinsically motivating, it's a good idea to recognize your achievements. Provide appropriate rewards as you make progress. In fact, establish a schedule of incentives that coincide with the bite-sized steps mentioned above. For example: **STRATEGY #6**

Short-range:

1. Get the class book(s).
   Incentive: Treat yourself to an hour of swimming.
2. Review the introduction and table of contents of the book(s).
   Incentive: You're already ahead of the game. Relax and enjoy the first day of class.
3. Carefully read the instructor's course description, assignment page, and any other handout.
   Incentive: Go for a leisurely walk around campus.

Mid-range:

1. Complete all assigned homework.
   Incentive: Once you have accomplished this each week, treat yourself to a movie or a special dinner.
2. Correct and rework any problems marked incorrect on homework or tests.
   Incentive: Get that new CD or book you've been wanting.
3. See the instructor at least once a week for extra help.
   Incentive: Get a pizza with a friend.
4. Find a study group (if this fits your learning style).
   Incentive: After each meeting, go to the student center to visit with friends.
5. Participate in class.
   Incentive: At the end of each week, make plans for a special getaway weekend at the end of the semester.
6. Get "As" on all the tests.
   Incentive: After each "A," plan an evening activity that's just for fun.

Long-range:

To attain an "A" in math by the end of the semester.
Incentive: Take your well-deserved long weekend of rest and relaxation.

W.I.N.

Lou Holtz, coach of the Fighting Irish of Notre Dame, is renowned for his football expertise. He is also a great motivator of student athletes. When confronted with a difficult choice, Coach Holtz instructs his players to follow the principle of W.I.N.—What's Important Now.

Every day, no matter how small or seemingly insignificant it may seem, take some step toward your goal. Ask yourself, "What's important now for me to achieve my goal?" Once you have identified the step, act on it. If you do not make progress towards your goal, no one else will. **STRATEGY #7**

OK. Let's put all this information to work. Take a moment now to work on Buddy's Goals.

BUDDY'S GOALS

Your best buddy has asked you to review the following list of personal goals. Put a check (✓) next to the items you think clearly state a goal. Put an "x" next to the items you think are not very clear.

1. I will do better in school next term.
2. I want to raise my math average by at least one letter grade.
3. I want to write something worthwhile in English class.
4. I need to remember more stuff.
5. I want my instructors to like me.
6. I will be able to write a clear thesis statement for every essay I am assigned.
7. I will study more effectively by appropriately rewarding myself each time I move closer to my goals.
8. I will be nicer to my family.
9. I will become a better friend.
10. I will become healthier by doing at least thirty minutes of aerobic exercise four days per week.

Take a moment, and jot down what was wrong with some of the goals you just reviewed. Pick one of the poorly written goals and improve it.

Now, assume the rewritten goal is your own. How are you going to be successful at achieving this goal? Write your plan below (briefly).

_____

_____

_____

_____

❖❖❖

It is obvious that Buddy's goals 1, 3, 4, 5, 8, and 9, while having worthwhile intentions, do not clearly prescribe a course of action. They are just too vague. For instance, Buddy can elaborate on goal 1 so that it reads something like:

Long-range:

I want to raise my GPA to a 3.2 by the end of the next term.

Mid-range:

I will review the notes from each class as soon after the class as possible.

I will participate in class discussions.

I will, when I have the choice, sit in a location with as few distractions as possible.

I will stay up to date with all my reading assignments.

I will not wait until the last minute to prepare for exams.

Short-range:

I will make sure I have all my academic tools—books, notebooks, pens, pencils, calculators, dictionary, and any other items required by my teachers. I will have these when the term begins.

Although items 2, 6, 7, and 10 can use some clarification, they are closer to the mark. They are much more specific.

Let's put all this to work for you before you move on to Chapter 3. Look at the challenges you identified on the Assessment of Strengths and Weaknesses in this chapter. Pick the two that give you the most difficulty. Write a clear goal for each. Remember to be specific and to include a road map (the mid-range and short-range goals).

- Next, identify two personal, non-academic desires you have. Write a clear goal for each. School is important, but it is *not* your whole life. Balance your activities.

- Once you have written your specific and measurable goals, post them in a place where you will see them every day: your mirror, computer terminal, dresser, refrigerator . . . . Look at them and remember the W.I.N. principle.

- Work on your goals with a buddy. Encourage, discuss, and generally keep each other on track.

Remember to look at the big picture. Imagine you *are* successful.

Evaluate your goals: Wanting to do something is not the same thing as doing something

Have you ever set a new year's resolution? "I will lose ten pounds this year." "I will go to the gym three times per week." "I will *really* buckle down and study this term." We've all made these—and we've all broken them. It's easy to make the resolutions, but much harder to live up to them.

Set aside time—say, once a week—and evaluate your performance. You've already written your goal and road map. Look at these. What kind of progress are you making? If it's minimal, why? Is the goal realistic? Are you making diligent effort? Maybe you need more resources.

STRATEGY #8

For example, maybe you would have a better chance of getting to the gym if you asked a friend to go with you. Or maybe you would do better in class if you got out of that study group—which has really become a *social* group.

Be aware of any distortion of thinking you might experience. Because you may have encountered some glitches does not mean you're a failure. Think of the successes and build on them. Adjust your course as necessary and focus on the next step on your road map.

"Failure is delayed success."—Thomas Edison

A QUICK REVIEW

As you get ready to tackle our next topic, remember that successful students:

- know their challenges as well as their strengths
- are shrewd and insightful
- give themselves breaks and rewards
- are proactive and can visualize success
- are justifiably confident (Each of us has a different sky)
- establish effective and efficient plans
- have goals that are written, specific, measurable, realistic, valuable, and have an end point (or as one of my seminar participants said, "a go-to point")
- take a step, no matter how small, each day toward the desired result
- periodically review your progress, either individually or with a friend, and revise as needed
- have goals that fit into an overall vision of academic or personal life

In other words, successful students see their academic progress as part of a grand scheme.

Focus on your goals—focus on success.

Summary of learning style correlations

Please remember to pick and choose among the strategies presented in this book. As you read in the Introduction, one size does not fit all. It will be your job to mix and match strategies to fit your particular learning style. Examples throughout this book are given of how the same topic can be successfully addressed by the auditory learner, kinesthetic learner, and visual learner. There are also reminders when it comes to the chapter topics and your learning environment. Please feel free to adjust as necessary. These should not be taken as unquestioned absolutes, but as practical suggestions to spark further thinking on your part.

TOPIC	AUDITORY	KINESTHETIC	VISUAL
Taking breaks	listen to music	move about; throw a football	look at a video, tv
Setting goals	tape record your goals and play them back	cut and paste; place on a cork board or magnetic board; move them about as priorities change	write the goals and post them in a conspicuous place

General comments about a learning environment:

- Establish a study space conducive to your needs (amount of light, temperature, and the like).
- Get a buddy to act as support personnel—unless your style is to work alone.

CHAPTER 3

SO MANY ASSIGNMENTS—
SO LITTLE TIME

- • Introduction
- • Goals
- ✔ **Time management**
- • Classroom expectations
- • Reading strategies
- • Writing and research strategies
- • Memory and relationships
- • Test preparation
- • Summary

1. **Get out of your own way**
   Goals give us purpose. Now let's organize time to accomplish the purpose.
   The Glitch Factor
   Let's take a look at your day
   What's eating your pie?
   Piscitelli's Prime Planning Principle = Simplify
   Backward planning
2. **It's a matter of priorities**
   Eighty percent of your results will come from twenty percent of your activities
   Urgent vs. Important
   Balance and moderation
   Calendars
   Long-term calendars
   Mid-range calendars
   Weekly planner
   Now, where did I put that calendar?
   How do I establish a study schedule?
   Efficiency vs. Effectiveness
3. **A quick review**

If you don't know where you are going,
you'll probably end up someplace else.

—Yogi Berra

GET OUT OF YOUR OWN WAY

In the last chapter, you concentrated on two major points. First, you want to become a successful student (or a more successful student). Second, written goals allow you to plan and measure specific progress. Students with clear goals empower themselves to be responsible individuals who no longer just react to their environment. Now, the successful student needs to become an effective planner who makes efficient and effective use of time.

Goals give us a purpose. Now let's organize time to accomplish the purpose.

The major premise of this chapter is simple: If only we can get out of our way, we will accomplish much more.

Did you ever wonder why students feel overwhelmed and swamped? Between class work, homework, after-school activities, family responsibilities, and personal activities, there are a lot of demands. The clock and calendar will always be there—like it or not. The key to managing time effectively is to understand what you need to accomplish. Anticipation will help to reduce your pressure and avoid crisis. Rather than doing everything (or most things) at the last minute, let's focus on our tasks, achieve results, and have time left for ourselves. You cannot control time. You cannot create time. But you *can* effectively use time for your benefit.

Well-laid plans, however, can also come crashing down around us. Have any of the following ever happened to you?

You *knew* it would take only thirty minutes to complete that math assignment. You're now into your second hour—and you're not done yet.

It's the night before that big report is due. You've done all the research, written the rough draft, and just about completed word processing. The power goes out/the printer gives you a foreign language/the hard drive crashes. You've got zip to hand in, and the teacher accepts no excuses.

I'm sure you can think of more. I cannot give you a foolproof/crisis-proof time management system. I'm not sure anyone can. But there is one characteristic—one general strategy—*successful* students use.

The Glitch Factor

 Successful students are flexible. They can adapt to changes and unforeseen events because they have built in a Glitch Factor. We'll read more on this later in the chapter. For the time being, just be aware that problems—glitches—do occur. Be prepared; anticipate a slowdown so that you can navigate around it. No matter what you have planned, try to give yourself some breathing room.

Let's take a look at your day

ACTIVITY

Draw a pie graph in the space below. The graph shown is only a guide. You can have as many divisions as apply to your situation. Each section of the pie represents an activity you generally do during the week. In a typical week (168 hours), it shows about how much of your time is devoted to sleeping, being in classes, doing homework, employment activities, doing chores, going to ball or dance practice, doing church-related activities, or anything else you do.

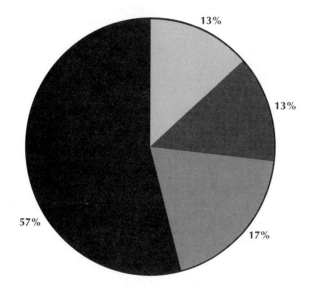

Use the space below to draw your graph.

By doing this activity, you become much more aware of how you use your time. How much of your time do *you* use in a productive manner? Are you surprised by the picture? Do you wish to change? Well, before you can do anything about *managing* your time, you must first specifically understand how you are currently using time—and how you *want* to use it. Take a moment to complete the next activity.

PROBLEMS IN TIME MANAGEMENT[10]

Listed below are some of the most common problems students face in trying to manage their time. Circle the ones that cause you problems in time management.

Assignments are too big to handle
Interruptions (like phone calls)
Watching too much television
Listening to too much radio/stereo
Meetings (school, youth groups, work)
Messy study space
No designated study space
Disorganization
Attempting to do too much
Lack of planning
Procrastination (waiting until the last minute)
Inability to say no when someone asks a favor
Unrealistic time estimates (expecting to finish a task in less time than it
  really takes)
Unclear instructions
Not listening carefully to teacher instructions
Others' mistakes
Socializing
Managing crises (emergency situations, urgent events)
Friends stopping by the house
Too much work to do
Others requesting my help
Lack of target dates/deadlines
Too many unfinished projects/tasks—lots of incomplete activities
Making careless mistakes so work has to be redone
Wanting my work to be perfect
My parents/roommate/family
Feeling stressed or overwhelmed
Too many different projects at the same time
Inability to make decisions
Working on trivial things rather than important ones—don't prioritize well
Fearing failure

Lack of balance—working too much
Lack of balance—playing too much
Lack of flexibility (ability to adapt to changes)
Lack of needed information
My sister/brother/children
Test-taking

Other:_____

_____

_____

_____

_____

_____

What did you discover about the manner in which you manage time?

Write your reactions below.

_____

_____

_____

_____

_____

_____

❖❖❖

A closer look at the above list indicates some very broad categories under which these challenges fall:

Poor communication
Poor ability to focus
Too many interruptions
Poor organization

Where do most of your shortcomings fall? What can you do about these? What would a successful student do?

What's eating your pie?

One more activity . . . this one requires that you identify those items that seem to cause the *most* problems for you with your time. That is, when you run out of time, what is it that has been eating up your pie? What has been wasting your time?

WHERE DID ALL MY TIME GO?

Did you ever start an activity—a homework assignment, a household chore, a favor for a friend—but for some reason, you never did complete it? You had the best intentions. You really wanted to finish the project, but before you knew it, there was no time left.

Why does this happen? Chalk it up to time-wasters. We are responsible for some; some come from other sources.

Recall occasions you ran out of time and then complete the following chart:

TIME-WASTER	WHO STARTED THIS TIME-WASTER?	HOW CAN *YOU* CONTROL THIS TIME-WASTER?
1.		
2.		
3.		
4.		
5.		
6.		
7.		
8.		

What conclusions can you draw from your responses? Write your reactions below.

_____

_____

_____

_____

_____

_____

Are you able to identify the worthless activities or time-wasting interruptions that keep you from being as successful as you want to be? The key to being a more successful student is to focus on your challenges (refer to Chapter 2). The challenges in this case are those activities you listed in the first column above.

True, you do not need to spend every waking minute of your day doing school work. We all need diversions to stay fresh. But when those diversions interfere with your progress, you must take a hard and honest look at them.

Now that the time-wasters have been identified, devise a plan to limit their negative effects. Here are a few solutions students have suggested:

TIME-WASTER	WHO STARTED THIS TIME-WASTER?	HOW CAN *YOU* CONTROL THIS TIME-WASTER?
1. **My friend calls me on the phone**	My friend	Tell my friend I'll call back after finishing my homework.
2. **Watching TV**	Me	Set aside time to watch TV after homework is complete; watch TV for a few minutes as a break during studies.
3. **Listening to the radio/stereo**	Me	Concentrate on my work; reward myself with a "radio break."
4. **Household chores**	My parents (or roommate)	Set up a schedule.
5. **Recreation**	My friends and I	Recreation is important, but I won't let it interfere with what I need to accomplish. Use a schedule.
6. **School**	Not me, that's for sure!	Watch it! The successful student sees school as a "positive"; there is a desire to do well. If I see school as a time-waster, I need an attitude check and adjustment.

You might recognize some of the time-wasters listed above; yours might be totally different. It really does not matter. What is important is that you've recognized interruptions interfering with your becoming that successful student. Now it's up to you to do something about these time-wasters.

TIP! On a 3" x 5" index card, list your three biggest challenges when it comes to time management. Use the activities above to help you focus. Now, write a goal that addresses each challenge. Put this card in your wallet, pocket, purse, or notebook. Refer to it at least once each day—and make sure you take at least one step toward that goal every day.

$$P^4 = S$$

Piscitelli's Prime Planning Principle = Simplify

STRATEGY #9 A major strategy for managing time is to look at the big picture, and then break down the overall task into smaller steps. Although the big picture is necessary in order to find our direction, it can be overwhelming.

One organization expert, Sara Gilbert, refers to this as the SOS principle: Simplicity, Order, Steps.[11] Simplify by breaking things down into small steps. Order your activities so you know what to do first, then second. Now take each step, one at a time, simple things first, until you reach your desired goal.

Let's relate this to a classroom assignment.

ACTIVITY

THAT INSTRUCTOR MUST THINK HOMEWORK IS ALL THERE IS TO LIFE.

Face it: homework is a fact of school. We may not like it. It may interfere with fun. But it does have a purpose. Homework gives you the chance to practice new skills, analyze information, and make mistakes. Yes, *make mistakes*. This is one of the best ways to learn. Correct the errors *before* the exam, and you improve your chances for better test performance.

With the right attitude, and plan, we might make homework easier to handle. We might even learn to like it. And you can still have plenty of time to pursue those personal goals you have established—remember them?

Let's try a little activity.

Your instructor has just assigned a major project. You have to write about the accomplishments of one of the emperors of ancient Rome. The assignment is due in three weeks. Briefly jot down the steps you would take to complete the assignment—that is, how you would manage your time.

How would you tackle this project? Write your plan below.

_____

_____

_____

_____

_____

_____

_____

_____

_____

❖❖❖

A list of small steps and personally imposed deadlines might include:

1. Look through your textbook to narrow down a list of possible emperors. (Day 1 and 2)
2. Go to the library with this "short list" and do some general research to select which emperor to write about. (Finish by day 4)
3. Gather your resource material. (By day 5)
4. Take notes. (Finish by day 9)
5. Develop an outline. (Day 10)
6. Write a first draft. (By day 13)
7. Revise and write a second draft. (By day 15)
8. Have someone proofread and comment. (By day 16)
9. Make final revisions of draft. (By day 18)
10. Turn in on time—in fact, finish a couple of days before the deadline. This takes into account the glitch factor. (Day 19)

Your list might differ, but you have established a flexible plan by which to operate.

Backward planning

Another strategy is to plan backwards. Suppose you have a test scheduled in one week. Let's start with the end product—walking into class prepared for the exam. Work backward—how will you get to this point? The following chart provides a quick guide.

STRATEGY #10

GOAL: TO RECEIVE AN *A* ON MY SCIENCE EXAM

DAY	TASK
Thursday	Successfully take science exam
Wednesday	Briefly review major topics. No cramming necessary
Tuesday	Review vocabulary and potential exam questions
Monday	Review notes again (reread)
Sunday	Review chapter questions in textbook. Try to identify potential exam questions.
Saturday	Review class notes; review vocabulary and study guide sheets
Friday	Review class notes; reorganize; write a brief summary of notes; provide a descriptive title for notes
Thursday	Make sure all textbook readings are complete

Once you have established your smaller tasks, you are ready to address the most important aspect of time management—prioritization.

IT'S A MATTER OF PRIORITIES

What is so critical about prioritizing (establishing an order of importance)? How does this tie in to time management?

The successful student realizes that certain tasks are more important than others. In fact, certain tasks must be completed before you can move on. A lack of prioritization will lead to wheel spinning—wasting your time. If you start writing a research paper before you establish a rough outline, you will not have direction. The final draft will reflect this lack of direction—as will your instructor's evaluation.

STRATEGY #11

One way to set priorities is to ask yourself this question once you have established your "to-do" list: "If I only had time to complete one activity, what would it be? Two activities? . . ."[12] This exercise forces you to focus on the issues of importance.

Be honest with yourself and remember the purpose of this book.

ACTIVITY

ESTABLISHING PRIORITIES OR
I FEEL OVERWHELMED. WHAT SHOULD I DO FIRST?

Most students think study skills will only be helpful in the classroom. Let's eliminate that erroneous perception. This activity is a modification* of the typical "let's-organize-our-homework" approach. I believe this is a super strategy for all aspects of life. Once you practice this a few times, you should see how obvious and easy it is to use. Use it daily, weekly, monthly, or in any manner appropriate for your purposes. **Focus** on your situation and adapt this tool. Make it work for you.

<u>ACADEMIC</u>

1: English
2: Math
3: Chemistry
4: Psychology
5: _____
6: _____
7: _____

PERSONAL

1: Clean my room
2: Write a letter to Uncle Bubba
3: Go shopping for new winter jacket
4: Practice my guitar
5: Establish an exercise program
6: _____
7: _____

What should I do first? I feel overwhelmed. The comparison chart below will allow you to **visualize** your tasks in an objective manner. Let's take the academic column first. Compare English with math. Which subject is more important for you to work with at this time? Circle either 1 or 2. Compare English with chemistry. Which is more important to you at this time? Circle your choice. Continue doing this for all of the numbers.

STRATEGY
#12

1/2	1/3	1/4	1/5	1/6	1/7
	2/3	2/4	2/5	2/6	2/7
		3/4	3/5	3/6	3/7
			4/5	4/6	4/7
				5/6	5/7
					6/7

(Obviously, you can do the same with the items listed under **PERSONAL**. You can even create another column in which you mix and match academic and personal tasks. Be creative.)

WHAT DO THESE CIRCLES MEAN?

Count how many times you circled each number.

Which did you circle the most? _____

the next most?   _____

the next most?   _____

the next most?   _____

the next most?   _____

the next most?   _____

the least?   _____

WHAT DO THESE NUMBERS MEAN?

You have just established an order—a priority—of tasks. Now you can **focus** on the most important and not get sidetracked by those of lesser importance. One note of caution: Use this as a guide to accomplish your goals—but remember it is OK to rearrange priorities as new circumstances arise. It's OK to be flexible.

*Adapted from Jack Sharpe's *Teachers As Advisors Manual*, Stanton College Preparatory School, Jacksonville, Florida.

Business people constantly have to think of the best ways to use their time. Why? Because time is money. Here is a thought to keep in mind when planning your activities. I've learned this from entrepreneurs, time management consultants, study skill experts, and also from personal experience:

Eighty percent of your results will come from twenty percent of your activities

Imagine that! Another way of looking at the same principle is that eighty percent of what we do, gives us only twenty percent of our results.[13] Sounds like a lot of needless energy is being expended. It could lead to nail biting, hair pulling, and generally a high level of stress. Learn to simplify.

If this is truly the case—and I think there is some real worth to this principle—think of the time you can save in your studies. I'd make an educated guess that some students put more time into homework than is really needed. I'm glad you enjoy the homework, but you might be better served if you reduced your expenditure of time on school work— still getting the same or better results—and left some quality time for yourselves.

But what is the trick here? Of course, it's identifying what the important twenty percent is. We'll address this in later topics of discussion. It will take practice to identify the pertinent material effectively—but once you do, there will be more precious time left for things to which you *really* want to devote energies.

Urgent vs. Important

Dr. Stephen Covey makes a simple yet powerful point in his *Seven Habits of Highly Effective People*: Our daily activities can be seen as either urgent (not urgent) or important (not important).[14] Those that are urgent cry out for immediate attention. An important task is one that leads us closer to our goal(s). (Once again, look at the goals you established in Chapter 1.)

Urgency and importance do not always mutually reinforce each other. Look at the following diagram.

URGENT AND IMPORTANT	IMPORTANT BUT NOT URGENT
URGENT NOT IMPORTANT	NOT URGENT NOT IMPORTANT

The key, according to Covey, is to get as many of your activities as possible into the "important but not urgent" box. Urgent and not important activities tend, in most cases, to be the agenda items of other people. In order to manage your time effectively, you need to concentrate on those activities that move you closer to *your* goal—not someone else's. Do you see how this very powerful strategy easily connects with some of the strategies we've already discussed?

For instance, if you wait until the last minute to do an assignment (urgent), you are in the business of crisis management and stress production. If limited study time is frittered away by someone else (a time waster), you are then concentrating on items (not important) that will not move you toward your goal. The important tasks move you closer and closer to your goals (W.I.N.).

It's easy to get caught up in someone else's important activities—if *you* allow it to happen. And many times we don't even realize this is happening. One effective strategy is to keep a diary of your activities for a week. Be honest with yourself. Keep a running log of *everything* you do and for how long you do it. Review it. Label the activities as *"urgent"* or *"important."* I think you'll be surprised at your findings. Your goal here is to fill your day with as many important activities as possible. Do what *you* need and want to do—and less of what others are demanding. In other words, act on your environment rather than reacting to it.

Balance and moderation

STRATEGY
#16 One last note on this balancing act: Recreational activities are important activities. Diversion and relaxation are vital—as long as they are done in moderation and do not interfere with your goals. You need to treat yourself to down time; get away from your books and study area every so often. These breaks keep you sharp, focused, and energized. Not only do you need to make a commitment to do your very best in school, you need to promise yourself to maintain a balance between work and play in your life. As Dr. Covey states, it is important to prioritize your time, *but* make sure you make time for your priorities.

The costs of being out of balance can be very high—and counterproductive to what you are trying to accomplish in the classroom. Frustration, anxiety, and stress are *not* what this book is about. Leave time in your life for you!

Calendars

Look at the three types of calendars I've provided for you. These came from a computer program. You can use forms available on computer disk or in the more traditional book format. The point is to use *some* form of calendar.

As you look at these calendars, a host of questions may come to mind. What is the purpose of using three calendars? Do you have to use three calendars? When should you review your calendar? Calendars are useful, but are there any tips on how to remember to look at the calendar?

Let's briefly address these and other concerns.

Long-term calendars

Yearly Planner

January

S	M	T	W	T	F	S
	1	2	3	4	5	6
7	8	9	10	11	12	13
14	15	16	17	18	19	20
21	22	23	24	25	26	27
28	29	30	31			

July

S	M	T	W	T	F	S
	1	2	3	4	5	6
7	8	9	10	11	12	13
14	15	16	17	18	19	20
21	22	23	24	25	26	27
28	29	30	31			

February

S	M	T	W	T	F	S
				1	2	3
4	5	6	7	8	9	10
11	12	13	14	15	16	17
18	19	20	21	22	23	24
25	26	27	28	29		

August

S	M	T	W	T	F	S
				1	2	3
4	5	6	7	8	9	10
11	12	13	14	15	16	17
18	19	20	21	22	23	24
25	26	27	28	29	30	31

March

S	M	T	W	T	F	S
					1	2
3	4	5	6	7	8	9
10	11	12	13	14	15	16
17	18	19	20	21	22	23
$^{24}/_{31}$	25	26	27	28	29	30

September

S	M	T	W	T	F	S
1	2	3	4	5	6	7
8	9	10	11	12	13	14
15	16	17	18	19	20	21
22	23	24	25	26	27	28
29	30					

April

S	M	T	W	T	F	S
	1	2	3	4	5	6
7	8	9	10	11	12	13
14	15	16	17	18	19	20
21	22	23	24	25	26	27
28	29	30				

October

S	M	T	W	T	F	S
		1	2	3	4	5
6	7	8	9	10	11	12
13	14	15	16	17	18	19
20	21	22	23	24	25	26
27	28	29	30	31		

May

S	M	T	W	T	F	S
			1	2	3	4
5	6	7	8	9	10	11
12	13	14	15	16	17	18
19	20	21	22	23	24	25
26	27	28	29	30	31	

November

S	M	T	W	T	F	S
					1	2
3	4	5	6	7	8	9
10	11	12	13	14	15	16
17	18	19	20	21	22	23
24	25	26	27	28	29	30

June

S	M	T	W	T	F	S
						1
2	3	4	5	6	7	8
9	10	11	12	13	14	15
16	17	18	19	20	21	22
$^{23}/_{30}$	24	25	26	27	28	29

December

S	M	T	W	T	F	S
1	2	3	4	5	6	7
8	9	10	11	12	13	14
15	16	17	18	19	20	21
22	23	24	25	26	27	28
29	30	31				

STRATEGY #17 This particular calendar allows you to record and view the big picture of your grading period, semester, or school year. At a glance, you are able to see what assignments, tests, commitments, and the like are scheduled. This helps plan your time accordingly so that you will not be caught at the last minute doing *urgent* business.

STRATEGY #18 Earlier, in this chapter, we talked about the Glitch Factor. Look at your calendar; carefully examine all your due dates. As you break your big tasks into little ones, leave yourself some breathing room. If an assignment is due on the 23rd of the month, why not shoot for a completion date of the 20th? If something goes wrong, you have given yourself at least three days in which to fix the problem. This helps you to avoid panic attacks and crisis management.

Mid-range calendars

SUNDAY	MONDAY	TUESDAY	WEDNESDAY	THURSDAY	FRIDAY	SATURDAY
	1	2	3	4	5	6
7	8	9	10	11	12	13
14	15	16	17	18	19	20
21	22	23	24	25	26	27
28	29	30	31			

S	M	T	W	T	F	S		S	M	T	W	T	F	S
					1	2							1	2	3
3	4	5	6	7	8	9		4	5	6	7	8	9	10
10	11	12	13	14	15	16		11	12	13	14	15	16	17
17	18	19	20	21	22	23		18	19	20	21	22	23	24
24/31	25	26	27	28	29	30		25	26	27	28	29	30	31

This type of calendar provides more space to make in-depth plans. This format allows you to write specific steps on the way to task completion. You can also more easily see other time constraints with which you need to deal.

Weekly planner

Weekly Planner

S	M	T	W	T	F	S
	1	2	3	4	5	6
7	8	9	10	11	12	13
14	15	16	17	18	19	20
21	22	23	24	25	26	27
28	29	30	31			

Sunday _____

_____

Monday _____

_____

Tuesday _____

_____

Wednesday _____

_____

Thursday _____

_____

Friday _____

_____

Saturday _____

_____

This format is the nitty-gritty of planning. Once the week is planned, establish a to-do list, and then prioritize the tasks. This is a basic building block for effective time management. You really don't need a form for this. A piece of notebook paper will work just as well. The point is to use something on a consistent basis.

Now, where did I put that calendar?

All the calendars in the world are useless if you do not look at them. Once you use them, it will become habit, a necessary part of your book bag. Here are suggestions I have heard from students to help remind them to look at the calendar:

- Put the calendar on your mirror, dresser, or someplace you always go to each day.
- Place the calendar on the floor by your bedroom door. You'll have to walk right over it when you leave for the day.
- Write down personal activities (parties, ball games) on your academic calendar. You'll be more apt to look at it if you are looking for fun dates.
- Work with a buddy. When getting used to the calendar, use the phone to call each other for a reminder to look at your calendar. Just don't let this become a time-waster!
- Get in the habit of reviewing the calendar at a regular time. For instance, I make sure to look at my calendar before closing my books for the evening. It gives me a last clear picture of what I need to tackle when I awaken. No surprises!
- You need to *want* to look at the calendar.

Whatever works for you—use it!

How do I establish a study schedule?

STRATEGY #21

When filling in your calendar for the week, block out periods of time for your homework. For those of you who juggle family, job, extra-curricular activities, and school work, this might be difficult. It might even seem impossible.

Here is a simple method I've seen work with extremely busy students. Identify the following:

How many courses are you taking?
What is the approximate amount of homework hours/course/week? (The rule of thumb is two to three hours of homework per one hour of class time.)
How much of your time is already committed (class, practice, job, family, exercise, and sleep)? Look back at your pie graph in the beginning of the chapter.
How much time is left? That's your study time.
Make adjustments as necessary.

This is a great activity to conduct *prior* to signing up for classes. You can *realistically* ascertain whether or not you will have time to pursue your academic and personal goals and responsibilities.

Efficiency vs. Effectiveness[15]

So, armed with calendars in hand, you are ready to do efficient battle with the world. Right? Maybe. Think book bags for a moment. They allow for ease in toting texts, notebooks, pencils, paper, a stapler, and even a hole punch. Everything in one compact area. This is efficient.

What happens, however, when you try to locate the small assignment pad or the lone piece of paper you just put in the bag? You know the pencil is at the bottom of the bag— somewhere! You have make efficient use of the bag by having all your materials close at hand—but you were not effective.

 This can happen to all of us, in or out of class. You might be doing things much faster, but going in the wrong direction. Don't let any tool, like a calendar or book bag, become the end result. Make sure it serves your purposes.

A QUICK REVIEW

You've completed two topics on your journey to becoming a more successful student:

1. Motivational goal setting allows you to establish a direction, course and end point for which to aim.
2. Time management provides the plan to reach the goal.

Successful students know how to:

- anticipate potential obstacles
- budget their time
- identify time-management problems
- develop a plan to control time-wasters
- simplify tasks
- establish priorities for long-range, mid-range, and short-range activities
- identify and fill their week with important activities
- establish a realistic study schedule
- maintain a balance in their lives between academic and personal issues

Yogi Berra's comment quoted earlier in this chapter is appropriate. If you do not know where you are going, you will get lost. Life can have a plan and still be adventuresome. Planning does not translate into rigidity. You can be efficient and still be spontaneous!

With this in mind, you are now ready for the classroom experience.

Remember the major premise of this book: **"You want to be a successful student!"**

Summary of learning style correlations

TOPIC	AUDITORY	KINESTHETIC	VISUAL
Using calendars	try a hand-held tape recorder	place priorities on index cards; physically shuffle and review cards; construct a computer-generated calendar	written calendar and notes with priorities clearly labeled; maybe draw pictures to highlight major events; a computer-generated calendar
Backward planning	after writing the plan, or while writing it, "talk" yourself through it	draw your plan	draw your plan or write the list

General comments about your learning environment:

- When scheduling your priorities, if at all possible, keep in mind whether you are a morning or evening person; schedule to meet your strengths.
- Are you more comfortable with a rigid format or a more free-form flexible format?

CHAPTER 4

THE CLASSROOM EXPERIENCE

1. What is that teacher doing in front of the classroom?
   Practice
   Teacher style and emphasis
   Identification of teacher style + expectations = classroom success
   I really want to pay attention in class—but it's not easy
2. What am I doing in the back of the room?
   A word about being cool
   Creating a positive classroom mood
   Active learning
   Is your notebook open, pen ready, and mind receptive?
   But how do I know what should go in my notes?
   Note-taking styles
   Now that you have your notes, what should you do next? Applying
     the 3 Rs
   Managing your studies with a notebook
   Do you know the vocabulary of the subject matter?
   OK—but I still don't get the big picture
3. A quick review

Great minds have purposes, others have wishes.

—Benjamin Disraeli

WHAT IS THAT TEACHER DOING IN FRONT OF THE CLASSROOM?

This chapter will explore the classroom experience. First, we'll take a look at the front of the room—what the teacher is doing and what the teacher's expectations are. Then we will take a look at the back of the room—what you are doing in class. Specifically, we will review strategies that will, if practiced, enable you to become a more successful student.

Practice

TIP! Practice is an important point to stress here. The strategies we have been examining, and will continue to examine, will do no good if they are not used. And not every strategy is for you. Pick and choose according to your learning style—but you must choose and then practice. A basketball coach may show you the best way to toss in a jump shot, a guitar instructor will show you chord fingering, and your teachers continually give instructions to help in the classroom. However, if you do not practice, you won't progress.

The same is true of study skills. Practice may not make perfect—but, as one of my former students once said, practice will make permanent.[16]

Teacher style and emphasis

Teachers come in all shapes and sizes—not appearance or body build but classroom styles.

Think of the various teachers you have had. Their styles have ranged from lecture, to question and answer, to group work, to lab work, to discussion, to seat work. And regardless of the method of presentation, each teacher also has a set of expectations for student performance. Some teachers emphasize minute details; others seek broad generalizations for application to new situations. One teacher may require you to "take ownership" of the class by being actively involved, while the next instructor wants you to be a passive receptacle diligently copying his words of wisdom

IDENTIFYING WHAT YOUR INSTRUCTORS WANT FROM YOU

Here is a sampling of teacher styles and expectations. Circle the ones that apply to your current instructors.

I have teachers who:

give lecture after lecture
expect students to participate in class
concentrate on group work
concentrate on in-class seat work
are sticklers for details like dates, formulas, and classifications
pay close attention to grammar and writing skills
very seldom assign any writing work
are very serious and allow no joking in class
are very serious but do allow for light-hearted moments
never accept an assignment late
accept assignments late, but with a penalty
do not seem to care about punctuality
always seem to go off on a tangent
are always on target, seldom straying from the topic at hand

TIP! If you are aware of your teachers' styles, expectations, and emphases, you are on the way to improved performance. Preparation for the class is more focused, and anxiety should lessen. For those of you who are able to pick your own teachers, knowledge of teacher methodology is a vital factor in determining your schedule—or at least it is for the successful student.

Identification of teacher style + expectation = classroom success

Take a moment now to complete the chart "Does Teacher Behavior Affect Your Behavior?" This is not an evaluation of your teachers, but rather another awareness-building activity for you. (Refer to the check list above to help you with the third and fourth columns.)

DOES INSTRUCTOR BEHAVIOR AFFECT YOUR BEHAVIOR?

COURSE NAME	INSTRUCTOR'S NAME	INSTRUCTOR'S STYLE (LECTURE, DISCUSSION)	INSTRUCTOR'S EMPHASIS (DETAILS, THEORIES, DATES)	YOUR BEHAVIOR (SKIP CLASS, SLEEP, PAY ATTENTION)

Look at the style and emphasis columns. Now look at your behavior. Are there any connections or relationships? Do you seem to be more on task in certain classes than others? If so, why? In which classes, if any, do you have the most difficulty staying on task?

❖❖❖

 If this has been an honest reflection, this information provides graphic proof of how teacher method ties in directly with student distractibility and performance. It's obvious that certain classes require more focused energy. This chart also says something about your individual learning style—that is, how you best learn. (Refer back to the Introduction.)

Here are some basic preparation strategies for all classes. Remember, the teacher is in control of the room. You can't control the teacher, but you *can* control the manner in which you respond (which may in turn affect how the teacher then responds to you).

STRATEGY #22   You don't like the teacher. He's boring, mean-spirited, and a difficult grader. If there is a personality clash with a particular instructor, sit back and evaluate the situation. Have you contributed to the problem? What can you do to change the predicament? A common approach is to withdraw from the class. While this may be appropriate in some instances, it tends to be an easy way out that masks some deeper challenges. Is the instructor a difficult grader, or is it that you lack some basic process skills? Be honest. Just because you got an "A" in the previous course does not mean you were challenged. Transferring to another instructor might be an attempt to beat the system. This might be the time to "suck it up" and learn those skills you will need—now and in the future.

The teacher seems to assign only "busy work." Always do your homework. Effective teachers give homework with a purpose. Just do it. You may not see the purpose, but that doesn't mean one doesn't exist. The ineffective teacher has no practical academic reason for giving homework. Do it anyway. This means doing your reading assignments. Just because you don't have to turn in an assignment does not mean it isn't homework. (Refer to the Lucy scenario on page 11.) The first step to effective studying is to complete your daily assignments. Studying requires ongoing review and diligence.

STRATEGY #23

- Even if you have no specific assignment, review your class notes and activities nightly. You'll know where you've been and where you are going the next day. Just because there is not a *new* assignment does not mean you do not have homework (more on this later).

- Although it sounds elementary, have all your "tools." An athlete would not think of going to baseball practice without a mitt or shoes. A band member does not show up for a performance without the proper instrument. Why, then, walk into class without a pen, pencil, paper, or whatever else the instructor expects?

- Bring a good attitude. Athletes psych themselves up for a game. Performing artists ready themselves for a performance. Think of each class as a contest or opening night. Be ready for it. Don't strike out; don't forget your lines. Remember, one of the characteristics of a successful student is the *desire* to do well.

If you follow these tips and strategies, you will see an improvement in both performance level and attention span.

Of course distractions occur. We can't always be on target. But if we continually "drift" from class, then some adjustments need to be made. Here is another self-assesment activity. See if any of these affect you.

I really want to pay attention in class—but it's not easy

The bell has just rung. You're in your seat. It's time to learn. The teacher starts the lesson and . . . you start to "drift away." You really want to pay attention, but it is so difficult.

ACTIVITY

WHAT CAN YOU DO TO FIGHT DISTRACTIONS?

First, let's list some reasons why you might start to daydream or get restless:

the student next to you is making noise
the teacher is boring
there is noise right outside the classroom window
you're hungry
you stayed up late last night to watch a movie
you're reading a note from your friend
you're writing a note to your friend

you don't understand the lesson

you've left all your class material (pencils, pens, paper, book) at home or in the car
or in a locker

you're thinking about the coming weekend

you don't know the answer to any of the questions the teacher is asking the class

a cute female/male is sitting next to you

a great sporting event is scheduled right after school

it's the last class of the day

Now that you have identified the distractions, what can be done to control them? List **your methods to overcome these distractions.** Keep in mind your learning style. Maybe the reason you have been distracted is that you are working against your individual and unique needs as a student.

_____

_____

_____

_____

_____

_____

_____

_____

Remember: focus on success—not excuses.

**STRATEGY
#24**

There is one overriding strategy to deal with classroom distractions—*concentration.* Always remember your purpose. Look for verbal and nonverbal clues from your teacher. Be an active participant—ask questions. By reviewing your notes and activities nightly, you can arrive at your own questions that relate to the material. Can you determine the big pictures? What point is the teacher trying to make? Listen to your classmates' questions and answers; they can have lots of interesting insights. Take good notes and then review those notes.

**STRATEGY
#25**

You can make distractions work *for* you. Allow yourself the luxury of accepting the distraction. Distracting thoughts can be merciless, continually nagging and interrupting. Once that thought intrudes, welcome it in. Say to yourself, "This is not the best time for me to deal with this distraction, but I'll listen for a moment." If possible, jot down the distraction on a piece of paper. For instance, "Call Joey tonight," "When do the Braves play next?" "I'm so bored with school!" Now you can let it go. You've mentally told yourself that you will address the issue later.[17]

**STRATEGY
#26**

Why not have some fun with the distractions? The teacher is droning on about the Civil War. Well, picture him out there on the battlefield putting all of the soldiers to sleep. Or, the student next to you is constantly sniffling. You can offer a tissue or ask for quiet. You can also play a game: How many new facts can you get from the lesson before the next sniffle?

Silly? Probably. But that's OK if you can get the most from your lesson.

Boredom is not an acceptable excuse to "check out"

You *will* run into boring and opinionated instructors. Resist the temptation to judge. Actively engage the lesson. Evaluate the presenter and/or his message at a later time.

STRATEGY #27

WHAT AM I DOING IN THE BACK OF THE ROOM?

A word about being cool

Try to imagine this: Visualize yourself as a teacher. You're in your classroom looking out at a room full of students. And every student behaves just as you do in class. Each student responds, acts, and writes as you do. Are you pleased with this picture? Be honest.

When a student responds to a teacher request with rude and inappropriate comments, the student is telegraphing several points to the teacher:

I am not a successful student
I am so insecure about my knowledge in this class that I have to put up this
    smokescreen to protect myself
I have no respect for the teacher
I am not cool

You see, if you *are* cool you don't have to make a point of showing it. Those who try to show they are cool just don't have it. Not only are you not cool, but you have placed yourself in a terrible position with the teacher. Remember that teachers are individuals with feelings and emotions just like students. If you constantly try to make them look bad, you are the one who will lose. Trust me on this one.

STRATEGY #28

Creating a positive classroom mood

The teacher is the professional responsible for developing a learning environment that is inviting and productive. But you are also important in this process. Watch the successful students in your classes for the following characteristics:

- They are punctual for class.
- They don't constantly watch the clock. You can't, no matter how much you want to, make those hands move any faster. You can't control or create time.
- They are involved in the class activities.
- They don't sleep in the back of the room or write personal letters.
- They don't do homework for another class.
- They ask appropriate questions. Asking, "What time does this class end?" is not pertinent to the material.

- They realize that an absence does not excuse them from the responsibility to do work they missed.
- They have an up-to-date assignment pad to keep track of all homework, projects, and exam dates.
- They almost always come to class prepared and ready to work.
- They don't start packing up their books before the class is over. The clock does not dismiss the student—the teacher does. Packing up early means you might miss an assignment or a last important point. At the very least, it's rude and insulting to the instructor.

Active learning

STRATEGY #29

You want to be an active learner in class. What does that mean? The key to success in the classroom is participation. Sit as close to the front of the room as possible. You want a ringside seat for questions, answers, and the general presentation. If you can discuss a concept, you have a much better chance of understanding it. If your teacher's style does not lend itself to class discussion, you can still be actively involved by anticipating the teacher's lecture, asking questions of yourself, and the like. But you need to remain focused. Easy? No. Beneficial? You bet! Remember the 80/20 principle? If you understand the big picture, the teacher's style, and the teacher's expectations, you'll recognize the important materials. If you understand the big picture, you won't need to write every word said by the instructor. The more you write, the more you've got to wade through to get ready for an exam.

Is your notebook open, pen ready, and mind receptive?

During study skill seminars, I deliver a mini-lecture of about five minutes. The students' task is to take notes on the important material.

STRATEGY #30

Although we do not have that option at this moment, there are some other strategies you can use to sharpen your note-taking skills. For instance, you can turn to an educational TV channel and take notes on the evening's presentation. Have a buddy or parent do the same thing. Compare notes. If you would rather work alone, tape the same presentation. Take notes, then replay the presentation. Did you miss anything? Or tape a teacher's lecture and follow the same procedure at home. (A word of warning: As a rule, I do not recommend taping teacher presentations. Very few students ever listen to the tape again. Taping also ignores the real issue—improving note-taking. This one activity is just an exercise. Always get the teacher's permission before taping a presentation.)

Look at the notes you wrote. How did you know what to write? How did you know what was important?

But how do I know what should go in my notes?

Most instructors will give clues. You must vigilantly look and listen for these guideposts. Maybe the instructor will write the major points on the board or an overhead transparency. This might take the form of an elaborate outline or just a few key words. Be sure to write these points in your notes—and leave room to add any clarifying teacher comments.

Although note-taking involves writing, don't forget to engage your ears. Listen—*really* listen. You may hear the instructor's voice become louder or softer at certain points of the presentation. Or he/she may pause for a long period of time. These are indications of emphasis—and, thus, significance. Include these in your notes.

Sometimes the hints are less subtle. A numbered list is a good indication a test item is about to be presented. ("There were three reasons why the Constitutional Convention was convened.") If the instructor says, "To conclude . . ." or "The main point of this is . . . ," I suggest you keep writing. The biggest clue is, "Be sure you know this for the test."

By staying current with your reading assignments (see Chapter 5) you will have a more accurate idea what the instructor deems significant or trivial.

Note-taking styles

Note-taking is a very personal activity. You have to organize your notes in a format that complements your learning style. Three very general styles are elaborated here. You may not find any of these particularly appealing. That's OK. But find a style that works for you and be consistent in its use.

The following examples come from a lecture on the 1992 presidential campaign. The topic is really immaterial. It could just as easily have been the success of the Beatles or reactions in the Krebs cycle.

If you learn best by using very structured and orderly models, the following style note format may be for you. Notice that this outline is organized with Roman numerals, capital letters, numbers, and lower-case letters. Each indentation represents a smaller classification (or information of lesser importance).

NOTE-TAKING: THE TRADITIONAL OUTLINE

I. Major presidential candidates in the 1992 election

    A. George Bush

        1. Political party

           a. Republican

        2. Most previous job

           a. President of the United States since 1989

           b. Vice-president of the United States, 1981-1989

        3. Major issue on which he campaigned

           a. Republican years in office led to prosperity and foreign respect

    B. Bill Clinton

        1. Political party

           a. Democrat

        2. Most previous job

           a. Governor of Arkansas

        3. Major issue on which he campaigned

           a. The economic recession

    C. Ross Perot

        1. Political Party

           a. Independent

STRATEGY #31

2. Most previous job
   a. Chief Executive Officer for his own business
3. Major issue on which he campaigned
   a. An alternative to the two traditional parties

Perhaps your learning style does not allow you to use the above note-taking strategy easily. You are not sure where the instructor is moving with the lecture—and it is extremely difficult to determine what is a subcategory of a larger category. In other words, you need a model that allows more flexibility.

Notice that the following model has the same basic information. If your learning style is such that pictures help you learn, why not put your notes in a picture-like (or graph-like) structure. It is also easy to add information when using this model; a simple arrow or line can be used.

STRATEGY
#32

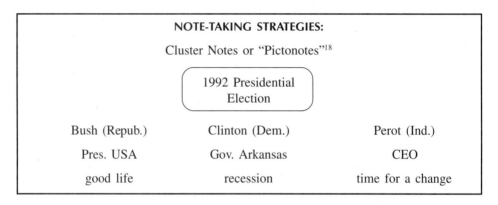

The following format is an adaptation of the Cornell Note-Taking System developed by Dr. Walter Paulk.[19] You will notice an expanded margin on the left side of the page for student questions or other organizing comments. This model is more linear in fashion than the preceding model, yet not quite as structured as the first model introduced.

STRATEGY
#33

TWO-IN-ONE NOTES

STUDY GUIDE	CLASS NOTES
Who were the candidates?	The 1992 presidential election
What parties were represented?	Bush: Republican president and former VP strong country for 12 years
What were the big issues of the campaign?	Clinton: Democrat governor of Arkansas economic recession
What kind of experience did each have?	Perot: Independent CEO of billion $ business alternative to Democrats and Republicans

There are probably as many organizing methods as there are students. Some students use the outline formats with numbers and letters. Others use the more free-flowing model depicted in the cluster note example. Here is one more.

This format[20] allows you quickly to arrange the *intricate parts* around the body of an *issue*.   **STRATEGY #34**

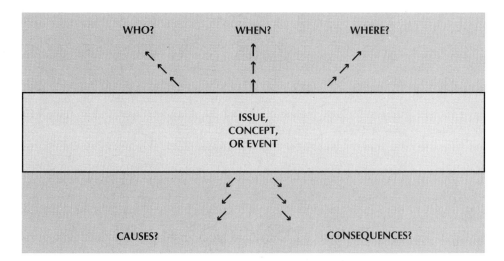

Even if you cannot take class notes in this manner, the above format allows for quick organization. It can be helpful in organizing your notes prior to a test, as well as in putting your thoughts together for an essay. This type of model might be what you need to jog your memory.

Here's an example:

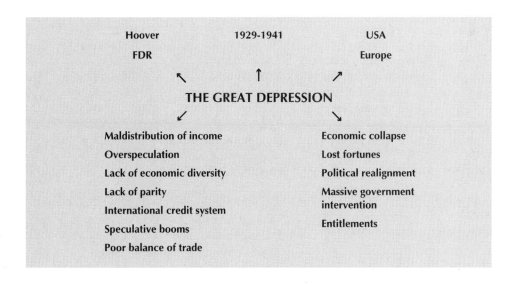

As with all models, this is a guide. You may have other items listed. Use these to brainstorm other events. The idea is to generate ideas, relationships and analysis.

 The note-taking style you choose is a personal thing. No one can tell you which one you should use. Pick one that fits your own learning style—and consistently use it.

For instance, if you are a very organized and linear thinker, the traditional outline (see page 55) might work best for you. It is structured. You can easily see what comes first, second, and so on.

If you tend to be more of a free-form or picture thinker, something like the cluster notes might be more fitting for you.

You can easily revise these styles to come up with your very own. Examine the notes you now take in class. Do they resemble one of the foregoing outlines? Is there any organization to your notes? If so, great! If not, develop one. Organized class notes will help you focus on teacher expectations and emphasis. Even if you feel notes are not needed in an easy class, take them anyway. You need the practice.

 Look at the Two-in-one Notes outline. This style, as indicated, provides space for a student-developed study guide. You can do this with any style you decide to follow. By preparing a study guide, you are developing possible test questions. In essence, you are actively engaged in organizing the information, while at the same time getting ready for the next test. (See Chapter 8.)

NOTE-TAKING STYLES: OVERVIEW OF PROS AND CONS

	TRADITIONAL OUTLINE	CLUSTER NOTES	TWO-IN-ONE
Pros	linear; structured; classifications and sub-classifications easily identified; may mirror the instructor's outline	more picture oriented; easier to add information at any time during the presentation by simply drawing a line to the appropriate spot; classifications can be seen easily; the tree-like format helps to visualize the "root" concepts	margin space for questions or reorganized outline; indentations still indicate classification levels

	TRADITIONAL OUTLINE	CLUSTER NOTES	TWO-IN-ONE
Cons	difficult to tell during a lecture where one classification begins and another ends; difficult to use with an instructor who tends to go off on tangents; not as easy to go back and add information during a presentation	too scattered for some students; can end up looking like a lot of crisscrossing lines	linear like the traditional outline; because of wide margin, less notes per page

Now that you have your notes, what should you do next? Applying the 3 Rs

Taking clear notes in class is one step closer to becoming a successful student—but there is more to do. Studying truly begins the next time you look at these notes. When should that be? As soon as possible after the class. Three strategies, the 3 Rs, will not only help you understand the material, they will cut down on last minute test preparation.

Review. Look at the class notes you wrote earlier in the day. Is there anything that is not clear? Do you understand all principles, generalizations, theories? If you have questions, put an asterisk or question mark in the margin of your notes. This should be your first question at the beginning of the next class meeting. You don't have access to the teacher the night before the unit exam. Also, by asking the question in class, you are actively participating—another one of our strategies. This is one of the "important" activities (see Chapter 3) to do each evening.

STRATEGY #35

Reorganize. As you look over your notes, look for a clearer way in which to see the big picture. Sometimes an instructor will present material out of order or will go off on tangents. Reshuffle your notes so they make sense to *you*. You may wish to write a brief outline in the margin of the notes (similar to those at the beginning of each chapter in this book). I ask students to come up with their own title for that day's class. If they can do this, they understand the big picture.

STRATEGY #36

One enterprising former student took class notes in various colored pens. She had developed her own system with each color representing a certain level/importance of information. Switching from pen to pen as I went from point to point was one of the most unorthodox strategies I have witnessed. It did, however, work for her. It helped with initial organization, as well as reorganization at a later date. Remember, pick and choose those techniques that best fit your style.

STRATEGY #37

STRATEGY #38

Relate. Students all too often attempt to memorize isolated pieces of information. This is a daunting, and boring task. Look at previous notes and reading assignments. Are there any connections? Do you see emerging trends or patterns? Once you start seeing this big picture, the material will make sense and become easier to remember. (See Chapter 7.)

STRATEGY #39

Adam Robinson, one of the innovators of the *Princeton Review,* recommends an interesting method. Each night, when you review your notes, transfer the main point or two, along with key concepts, to another sheet of paper. Continue to reorganize and relate each night in this manner. By test time you should have only one or two pages of notes. No more cramming for the exam! You have developed an ongoing study guide. *Note-taking is a vital part of test preparation.*

Managing your studies with a notebook

Great notes are useless if you cannot find them. Use a notebook for organization. The following guide has been used successfully by students. A well-organized notebook is extremely useful to study for finals, national exams (such as those administered by the College Board and the Educational Testing Service), or even in future courses.

STRATEGY #40

Your notebook can and should be a vital learning tool for you. The key is found in one word: organization. Get rid of those "stuff-it-in-the-pocket" folders that often tend to be agents of chaos. They may be efficient, but they are not necessarily effective. (See Chapter 3.)

The following are some pointers students have found helpful:

- Keep a separate three-ring binder for each class. It's frustrating to find English notes buried in the midst of information on the life of the Roman emperors. Keep all class notes separate.
- Place the course name, classroom number, time of class, and your name on the front cover.
- The first section of the notebook should include all general, yet important, handouts. This may include a course description, a listing of term assignments, and/or a class schedule of homework.
- Create a separate section for each unit of material. It may be helpful to divide each unit with a tab divider so that it will be easy to find the material. Each unit may look something like:

    summary outline or study guide for the entire unit
    daily notes with the date of each class (written in the upper right-hand corner)
    handouts that pertain specifically to that unit
    quizzes and other graded assignments
    the unit exam

- File all papers—do not just stick them in the notebook or textbook. There should always be an established order to follow.
- Keep a grade sheet. It can be a simple three-column format:

Assignment	Points Earned	Points Possible

Make the notebook work for *you*. Keep it current and review it every night. An orderly notebook says something about your seriousness and dedication to the course, and it helps you prepare daily for your next exam. This in turn will reduce test anxiety. (See Chapter 7.)

• Your instructor may have specific notebook requirements for his/her class.

Do you know the vocabulary of the subject matter?

Every discipline has its own unique way of speaking. Familiarity with the jargon of your courses will serve three purposes. You will have greater comprehension of the reading assignments; you will read at a more rapid pace; and you will follow the instructor's lecture more accurately. Here are some examples of discipline-specific vocabulary:

STRATEGY #41

English: metaphor, simile, denouement, plot
Math: polygon, theorem, congruent, exponent
Biology: phyla, kingdom, system, asexual reproduction
Geography: isthmus, continental drift, climate, culture hearth

There is also overlap of terms from discipline to discipline. Apply, evaluate, compare and contrast, analyze, and explain are used in all courses. (For a lengthier list of such words, see the essay guidelines in Chapter 6.)

Once you have determined the jargon of the discipline, keep a running list of new words—and make this a permanent part of your three-ring binder.

OK—but I still don't get the big picture

Even the best note-taker can be overwhelmed by a mountain of information and miss the big picture. Use the following strategies in conjunction with the 3 Rs we talked about earlier.

Work backward. First identify the major facts of the lecture, now the major issues, then the big picture. Finally, try to write a thesis statement about the material. Capture the essence of the lecture.

STRATEGY #42

Here are some sample lecture notes from an Introduction to Education class on the topic of the characteristics of an effective teacher.

After reading these notes, circle the major facts of the lecture, then underline any major issues. Finally, write a statement that effectively underscores the main point of the presentation.

I can't tell you how to be an effective teacher. I hope I have modeled some activities or behaviors that you will want to duplicate in your classroom. There is no one way to teach. We all have to adopt different approaches to fit our personalities. As long as you remain the child's foremost advocate, you should do well.

Here are a few styles. You have seen them all, I'm sure, from time to time.

Instructor-centered: Teacher is the imparter of knowledge; he is the model for the students to follow. The emotionally exciting educator will keep the kids on the edge of their seats. The emotionally sterile teacher will keep the kids on the edge of their sleep!

Content-centered: This type of teacher believes the content is the end-all and be-all of education. Instruction is determined by the text, subject matter, and curriculum.

Student-centered: The role of the teacher is that of facilitator. Developing inferential abilities in the students is considered vital. The teacher will use inquiry, discovery discussion, simulations, values clarification, brainstorming, and independent study. Learning contracts may be an integral part of this approach.

The Best Style? Keep one thing in mind: variety. Try to vary your teaching style from day to day—even within one class period. This will help the students—and you. You elementary school teachers know what I am saying better than anyone else.

Classroom observations: Look around your school. Who is doing what? Visit classrooms. Talk to the master teachers. You'll know who they are. Be big and accept the fact that you can learn from a colleague.

Perhaps you identified the following:

Major concepts: instructor-centered teaching, content-centered teaching, student-centered teaching.

Major issues: Teaching is a highly personal activity. Variety of style is important.

Thesis: Although no one can tell me how to teach, there are a few basic methods I should use on a regular basis to hold the interest of my students.

STRATEGY #43   Title/Summary/Concepts (T/S/Cs). A variation of the strategy above is to start by giving the notes a title, followed by a one-or two-sentence summary. Then list three facts that would support your summary. (This will be a great base on which to build the writing skills we will discuss in Chapter 6.)

Again using the sample lecture above, you might develop the following:

T: What is effective teaching?

S: Although no one can tell me how to teach, there are a few basic methods I should use on a regular basis to hold the interest of my students.

Cs: instructor-centered teaching, content-centered teaching, student-centered teaching.

STRATEGY #44   Prioritize the new information. What seems to be important based on past classes, teacher emphasis, and text readings? Is there a potential exam item here? (See Chapter 7.)

In the example above, students would've picked up on the fact that the answer to "What is the best teaching style?" is left up to them. This clearly correlated with my style throughout the semester (which is one of the issues we stressed in Chapter 3). Their priorities would be to identify the types of teaching styles and then to connect them to an overall philosophy of teaching.

Look for groupings and connections. Attempt to establish categories of data. For instance, if you're given a list of twenty-five items to remember, "chunk" the terms into three or four major categories.

STRATEGY
#45

In a history class, it might be helpful to group philosophers, scientists, and political leaders. Or how about the French vocabulary list below?

aimer mieux (v)	lorsque (adv)
l'anorak (n)	le peuple (n)
le bateau (n)	porter (v)
bientôt (adv)	prochain (adj)
célébrer (v)	puissant (adj)
le danger (n)	le roi (n)
la devise (n)	tricolore (adj)
entouré (adj)	

Rearrange according to parts of speech.

Nouns	Verbs	Adjectives	Adverbs
l'anorak	aimer mieux	entouré	bientôt
le bateau	célébrer	prochain	lorsque
le danger	porter	puissant	
la devise		tricolore	
le peuple			
le roi			

Now, instead of learning fifteen isolated items, you have "chunked" the material into four bite-sized categories of fewer words, each category with no more than six words.

"I've tried all this stuff, but I still don't understand the new math formula." Well, the good news is you have at least identified what you do *not* know. Try to "talk" a math problem through step by step. If possible, do this with someone who is not knowledgeable about the topic. This will force you to explain each step fully. The best way to learn something is to teach it.

STRATEGY
#46

ACTIVITY

Pick a topic (any course) you are currently studying and having difficulty understanding. Explain it in writing below step by step. Then explain it verbally. Draw a picture if it helps. Get into the essence of the topic.

Topic with which I am struggling:_____

_____

My step-by-step explanation:_____

_____

_____

_____

_____

_____

_____

What am I still unsure about when it comes to this topic? (Be specific and then ask your instructor if you cannot find the solution anywhere else.)

_____

_____

_____

_____

_____

❖❖❖

A QUICK REVIEW

Before we go any further, let's review what you have covered in these first four chapters. Let's apply one of the strategies you have learned in this chapter. For each of the following points, write a one-sentence summary of its contribution to better academic performance:

1. *Motivational goals* _____

    _____

    _____

2. *Time management* _____

    _____

    _____

3. *Teacher expectations* _____

    _____

    _____

4. *Clear and organized notes* _____

_____

_____

Compare your answers with those below:

1. **Motivational goals:** A clear plan of what I want, when I want it, and how I am going to get it! (I want an "A" on my science research paper.)
2. **Time management:** Learning to plan, organize and make efficient use of time. (First I will narrow my topic, then I will do initial research followed by a rough outline. After more research, I will write the first draft and have a friend review it.)
3. **Teacher expectations:** The teacher's style and expectations will directly affect my performance. I need to focus. (I will be thoroughly familiar with teacher guidelines and requirements for the project.)
4. **Clear and organized notes:** I need to understand the big picture; review, relate, and reorganize. (I will continually review, relate, and reorganize as I gather more information.)

Let's use an analogy of taking a trip to review our topics.

Motivational goals help identify the direction in which you wish to travel. You need to know where you are going.

Time management provides the plan of how to get to your desired destination.

Identifying the *expectations* of the people with whom you are traveling (working) is necessary preparation for the journey so you can get the most from the experience.

Effective notes of the journey allow you to "revisit" any time you choose without having to repeat a lot of hard work.

In other words, successful students are able to do the following in and out of the classroom:

- identify and work with teacher expectations
- adjust to varying teacher styles
- review class activities (lecture notes, video presentation, oral reports) each night
- relate and reorganize new information each day
- quickly and effectively deal with distractions
- actively and appropriately become involved in class activities
- ask appropriate questions
- keep track of all homework assignments
- pick and consistently use an effective note-taking strategy
- keep an organized notebook

Now let's turn to a topic every successful student must tackle—how to get through a boring textbook. Staying with our travel comparison, if you want to reach your destination you have to be able to read the road signs along the way.

Summary of learning style correlations

TOPIC	AUDITORY	KINESTHETIC	VISUAL
Teacher style	lecture is probably best	physical manipulation	demonstration
Avoiding distractions	ask questions and participate	hold something in your hand (like a bean bag) —but don't let it become a distraction	focus on the process of writing notes; draw when appropriate to illustrate notes
Note-taking	traditional outline —or some variation— may work the best	flash cards or index cards that can be manipulated and sorted	illustrated notes; maybe put word description on one half of page and drawings on the other; "organized doodling"
3 Rs	tape the salient points and play back; explain your notes to a buddy; discuss the material in a study group	as you're reviewing, it may be helpful to walk about the room; physically reshuffle the notes; watch a video to reinforce the notes; do an experiment when appropriate; whenever possible, "do" something rather than just "writing" something	make margin outlines in your notes; draw flow charts and timelines; watch a video

General comments about your learning environment:

- Seat location is critical: remember to seek lighting and temperature appropriate to learning style.
- Bring a sweater to class; dress in layers.
- When possible choose an instructor suitable to your style.
- Come to class hungry or full, whichever is better for you.
- If possible, schedule classes to coincide with your energy levels.
- Try to schedule study time during an optimum time of day.

CHAPTER 5

I HAVE TO READ 1,000 PAGES BY WHEN?

- Introduction
- Goals
- Time management
- Classroom expectations
- ✔ **Reading strategies**
- Writing and research strategies
- Memory and relationships
- Test preparation
- Summary

1. Reading with a purpose
  I read my assignment. So why don't I know what I read?
  Identifying the purpose
  Tackling a reading assignment
2. Dealing with a boring textbook
  How does the instructor expect me to get through this boring
    textbook?
  The plan
  The "tangential" instructor
  Guarantees?
  Now what?
  My instructor always falls behind schedule.
  I've followed the plan, but my reading comprehension is still lousy!
  The reading plan is fine for textbooks—but what about novels?
3. A quick review

That must be wonderful;

I have no idea what it means.

—Moliere

READING WITH A PURPOSE

It's happened to all of us. You did your homework reading just like the teacher asked. But you simply did not remember what you just read. Or you did not know what material was most important. So you tried to remember everything, you got overwhelmed, and you feel as if you wasted your time. That's as frustrating as studying for an exam and still getting a poor grade.

I read my assignment. So why don't I know what I read?

If you were asked to clean the garage (or your room or the backyard or the kitchen), would you just start working anyplace, moving anything? Probably not. You might ask what your final result was to be. Or you might want to know exactly what should be moved, thrown away, put away, or cleaned. In other words, you would want to know what the *purpose* or *end result* of your work should be.

The same holds true for reading. Here are some hints:

Why do we forget what we read? Recognize the following reasons—and try to do something about them:

- you did not understand the material
- you did not learn earlier material
- you did not know what to remember
- you did not have the right attitude when reading
- you got bored
- you read inefficiently
- you could not establish relationships
- you did not have an adequate vocabulary to understand the material

Take a deep breath. You cannot possibly (nor do you want to) memorize everything you are reading. Remember that your initial reading of an assignment is not the same as studying. When completing your assignment, you are trying to get an understanding of the *big picture*. Don't get caught in the trap of trying to play Trivial Pursuit with your reading.

STRATEGY #47   *Different books require different reading strategies.* A science book with lots of facts and a strange vocabulary is not to be read like your history text or a good novel. Recognize the differences and make adjustments. The key to increased reading comprehension is to know what the end result should be. There are, essentially, six purposes or reasons for reading.[21] It does not make sense to read everything in the same manner. Different books require different strategies. The six purposes are:

1. to get a message
2. to find details
3. to answer specific questions
4. to evaluate the reading material (make a judgment)
5. to apply the reading material (use it in new situations)
6. to entertain

• *Give yourself plenty of* **appropriate** *breaks* so you do not become exhausted.

• *Stay* **focused.**

Identifying the purpose

The $64,000 question is, "How do you know what the purpose is?" Well, if you have been paying any sort of attention in class, this will not be a problem. The teacher almost always gives clues. The textbook will also. Remember the 80/20 principle? Well, let's apply it here.

You have a fifty-page reading assignment from your history instructor tonight. That's a lot to read. But if eighty percent of what you need to know is in approximately twenty percent of the pages, you have just cut your reading to ten pages. If it takes you three minutes to read a page, you have just saved yourself two hours of work! Let me illustrate with a personal example.

STRATEGY #48

Among the courses I teach is United States History. My emphasis is to show students developing relationships throughout our nation's political, social, and economic development. One area to which I have never given much class time is military history. Right or wrong, this has not been an emphasis in my courses.

Now, one chapter of a recent student text consisted of twenty-five pages covering the years 1861-1865. Fifteen of the pages (sixty percent of the total) dealt with Civil War military campaigns. The successful students recognized this fact and did not concentrate on those pages. They gave more time to the political and social consequences of those years.

If you can recognize this from the outset, there is less of a chance of being overwhelmed by extraneous data. As you go further in school, more will be expected and assigned. Learn now how to take well-calculated short cuts. Please do not equate this with the "easy way out." It is, however, a more efficient manner to attain your goals.

Another example: If I asked you to find the phone number for Mr. Dominic Jones at 123 Maple Lane, what would you do? Would you pick up the phone book and start reading from the As? I doubt it. Why not? Because it would be a waste of your time. You would scan for the Js, and then scan for his name until you found it. Why read what is not necessary? The same principle should hold true for your school assignments. This is a skill that can be used beyond school—on your job, in your pleasure reading, or in deciding on a vacation spot.

STRATEGY #49

Tackling a reading assignment

Before beginning practice or entering an actual game situation, athletes warm up. They perform calisthenics and stretching exercises to limber up their muscles.

Reading should be no different. If you just open your book to the assigned page and start reading, you have, in effect, started running without warming up. Don't be a passive reader—mindlessly going through the motions as you drift from page to page like a leaf blown by the wind. Move with a purpose!

DEALING WITH A BORING TEXTBOOK

Unfortunately, most textbooks are dry and sleep-inducing. One would think authors get a bonus for writing boring and encyclopedic volumes. But your teacher will expect you to read the assignments.

What is a student to do?

How does the instructor expect me to get through this boring textbook?

If you are like most students, you probably have asked this question many times during your school years. It will not be easy, but if you follow the plan listed below, you will not only "get through" the dusty textbook, you will also retain more than you ever thought possible. And if this works for boring books, think of the results with exciting works you *want* to read.

"Sometimes, the only difference between a sleeping pill and a textbook is that the textbook doesn't have a warning label about operating heavy machinery."[22]

Before I get to the plan, let me remind you of one of our goals:

> You wish to study more efficiently.

It is all about the right attitude. *You* need to make the commitment—and then stick with it. There is nothing magical about this approach. I have used it with my students since becoming a classroom teacher. Others[23] have written about it. It is a common-sense approach successful students have used for years. But if you lack the desire, you won't accomplish it.

Take a moment to complete the following activity. Pull out one of your textbooks in which you currently have a reading assignment. Below, write the steps you normally would take to complete the assignment. When you have finished this, read my plan.

ACTIVITY

Date:_____

Class:_____   **The assigned pages:** _____ **through** _____

My steps to successfully completing a reading activity:

*Step 1*_____

_____

*The next step*_____

_____

*The next step*_____

_____

*The next step*_____

_____

*The next step*_____

_____

*The next step*_____

_____

*The next step*_____

_____

*The next step*_____

_____

❖❖❖

The Plan

More than five decades ago, F.P. Robinson developed a reading strategy that has been duplicated ever since. The technique, known as SQ3R (survey, question, read, review, recite), is the basis for the following plan. Most study skills books have some variation of this plan. Call it what you will, there are essentially three stages to the plan: pre-read, read, post-read.

Pre-Read

STRATEGY
#50
1. You have to know the purpose. Do you have a target? Or are you just wandering through the passage to finish? If you sit down to read your assignment but have no earthly idea why you are reading or what you are looking for, you might as well turn on the television and watch a football game. If you don't know what to look for, why bother torturing yourself? (Of course, the successful student would not give up.)

Ask some basic questions before starting. For instance, "What is this instructor concentrating on in class?" Or, "What kind of test items might come from this reading?" "I have to read because it's assigned" is *not* a purpose.

STRATEGY
#51
2. Warm up your intellectual muscles. Establishing a purpose is essential. Now stretch those mind muscles. You need to prepare actively to read. To accomplish this do the following:

Sit on the edge of your seat (literally). This sends a signal that you are ready to engage actively in work.

Quickly review in your mind (or by opening your class notes) what you have covered in class to date on the topic before you in the text.

Relate as best you can, before you start reading, how this material might connect to the overall emphasis in the classroom. In other words, you should warm up by using past knowledge to ground you in the reading *and* to establish memory hooks for this new material. (More on this in Chapter 7.)

STRATEGY
#52
3. Skim and scan. Still warming up, quickly flip through the pages of the assignment. Skimming provides a quick feel for what the big picture is. What you want is a general sense of the assignment. Don't get caught up in a game of Trivial Pursuit. Read the introduction and summary of the chapter. Unlike a murder mystery, you *want* to know where you are going before you start. If you have to accomplish a certain outcome by the end of your reading—say, answer teacher-provided questions—then scan the material for this particular purpose.

STRATEGY
#53
This strategy, though it adds a little time to the front end of your reading, will aid comprehension and trim time from the overall reading assignment. Once you finish this pre-reading activity, you will have a better idea what you need to read—and what you can skip! (Remember the 80/20 principle.)

Skimming includes the following steps:
-Read the chapter headings/subheadings. Form questions from the headings. These questions will give you a *purpose* for reading. You will be actively looking for information.
-Look at all pictures, graphics, and captions. The author put them in the text for a reason.
-Look at bold-faced terms. They are highlighted for a purpose.
-Look at the end-of-chapter terms and/or questions (if available).
-Read the chapter's introductory section and summary.

Look at the following page from a psychology textbook.[24] These are the actual chapter headings and subheadings. As you read these chapter guideposts, ask yourself, "How would I use this information? What type of questions can I form from this information?"

What is Psychology?
Psychology as a science
What psychologists do
Clinical and counseling psychologists
School and Educational psychologists
Developmental psychologists
Personality, social, and environmental psychologists
Experimental psychologists
Psychologists in industry
Where psychology comes from: A brief history
Structuralism
Functionalism
Behaviorism
Gestalt Psychology
Psychoanalysis
How today's psychologists view behavior
The biological perspective
The cognitive perspective
The humanistic-existential perspective
The psychodynamic perspective
Learning perspectives
The sociocultural perspective
Human diversity and psychology
Ethnic diversity: A social mosaic
Gender
Other kinds of diversity
The diversity of contributors to the development of psychology
Critical thinking and psychology
Principles of critical thinking
Recognizing common fallacies in arguments
Summary

That's quite a reading assignment. Rather than run away, let's tackle this task with purpose and effectiveness. Here are some questions I developed using the above headings.

What is Psychology?

Psychology as a science
What makes psychology a science? What does it share with other sciences?
What does it attempt to do?

What psychologists do
What *do* they do? Are there different types of psychologists? How do they differ?
How are they the same?

Clinical and counseling psychologists
What do these psychologists do? Who do they counsel? What are their goals?

School and educational psychologists
What is the function of a school or educational psychologist? Are they in all schools?
What are their goals? How do they compare with other psychologists?

Developmental psychologists
What do they develop?

Personality, social, and environmental psychologists
What do these types of psychologists study? What is the difference between a personality
psychologist, a social psychologist, and an environmental psychologist?

Experimental psychologists
What types of experiments do they do? Why do they do experiments?
On whom do they experiment?

Psychologists in industry
Why does industry need psychologists? What do they do?
How are they different from the other psychologists?

Where psychology comes from: A brief history
When did psychology start as a subject?
Why did it evolve into an academic discipline?
What factors influenced its development?

Structuralism
What is structuralism? With what "structures" is it concerned?
Who developed this?

Functionalism
What is functionalism? With what "functions" is it concerned?
Who developed this?

Behaviorism
What is behaviorism? With what "behaviors" is it concerned?
Who developed this?

Gestalt Psychology
What is gestalt? With what is it concerned? Who developed this?

Psychoanalysis
What or who is being analyzed? Who developed this?

How today's psychologists view behavior
Who are today's psychologists? What behaviors are they viewing?
Why are they viewing this behavior?

The biological perspective
What is the connection between biology and psychology?

The cognitive perspective
What does cognitive mean?
Is there a connection between cognitive and biological perspectives?

The humanistic-existential perspective
What is the humanistic-existential perspective?
When and why did this perspective develop?
What does it do differently when compared to the other perspectives?

The psychodynamic perspective
What is the psychodynamic perspective? Why is it used? Who uses it?

Learning perspective
Is this perspective related to school and education?
Are only teachers concerned about it? Does it examine all forms of learning?

The sociocultural perspective
What does culture have to do with psychology?
If psychology deals with the mind, why are we looking at society?

Human diversity and psychology
Does this mean psychology is different when studying different groups
in our society or throughout the world?

Ethnic diversity: A social mosaic
Do ethnic groups have differing psychological makeups?

Gender
Are men and women psychologically different? If so, how?
Can I use psychology to find a husband/wife?

Other kinds of diversity
What other kinds of diversity exist? What is the connection to psychology?

The diversity of contributors to the development of psychology
Who have been the contributors to psychology? What did they contribute?

Critical thinking and psychology
What is the relationship between critical thinking and psychology?

Principles of critical thinking
What is critical thinking? Who uses it? Can I use it?

Recognizing common fallacies in arguments
What does fallacy mean? What do fallacies have to do with psychology?

Summary
Can I summarize what I just read? What are the main points? Can I write a brief conclusion
about all of this material? Can I participate intelligently in a class discussion on this chapter?
What were the most troubling concepts? What questions do I need to ask my instructor?

Yes, these strategies will shorten reading time. Any new skill is awkward at first. It
takes practice for it to become habit. Comprehension increases with more effective reading strategies. Yes, it might be difficult at first, but you must want it—desire is important
for the successful student.

Pause for a moment and develop your own questions for the following headings found
in a biology textbook.[25] You will find some potential questions in Appendix B.

INTRODUCTION

Fundamental concepts of biology

Your questions:_____

_____

_____

Evolution and natural selection

Your questions:_____

_____

_____

Adaptations

Your questions:_____

_____

_____

Energy and natural selection

Your questions:_____

_____

_____

Scientific method

Your questions:_____

_____

_____

Observations and hypotheses

Your questions:_____

_____

_____

Experiments

Your questions:_____

_____

_____

Limitations of experiments

Your questions:_____

_____

_____

Correlation studies

Your questions:_____

_____

_____

It's a fact?

Your questions:_____

_____

_____

Humans and environment

Your questions:_____

_____

_____

Summary

Your questions:_____

_____

_____

❖❖❖

4. Give yourself some tasks. You need to spice up the chore of book reading. Send yourself on a fact-finding mission. What is the important stuff? Use all clues that have been provided. If you are given a study guide—use it! If not, make your own. You have already turned all those chapter headings and subheadings into questions. (See pages 75–77.) This gives you a purpose, as you now must answer those questions. Review captions

STRATEGY #54

and graphics. Look at the end-of-chapter terms. In short, ask yourself, "What do I need to know?" Be an investigative reporter and ask who? what? when? why? where? how? Refer to the 80/20 principle. Obviously, class attendance will help here. (See how it all fits together?)

Read

STRATEGY
#55

5. Finally you are ready to read. It is one thing to do all of the preparation work called for in steps one through four, above, but it is quite another to take notes of the reading. "Just write good notes on the main points" doesn't help if you cannot figure out what the main points are in the reading section. A couple of suggestions are particularly pertinent at this juncture of your reading assignment.

- Refer to the questions you posed in step three, above. For instance, "What makes psychology a science?" As you read, jot the main factors that make this social science a discipline. Can each part be further subdivided? If so, make a note. Think of this process as the reverse of the writing process. Instead of building a body around a skeleton (the outline), you are picking the meat (main points) from the bones.
- If you generally have difficulty understanding the gist of an assignment, read one section at a time. Stop after each section and write a brief summary. Start with one paragraph, and move on to longer sections as you become more proficient.
- You may even decide to clump two or more headings together in order to develop relationships. "What psychologists do" can easily be grouped with any one (on all) of the following sections: "Clinical psychologists," "Educational psychologists," and 'Development psychologists." Your comparison could take the form of either cluster notes (see Chapter 4) or a data retrieval chart (see Chapter 7).
- "This sounds easy, but how do I know what the important terms are?" Mortimer J. Adler and Charles Van Doren, in their classic work *How to Read a Book,* guide you in the following fashion:

  If you do not fully understand the passage, it is probably because you do not know the way the author is using certain words. If you mark the words that trouble you, you may hit the very ones the author is using specially. . . . From your point of view as a reader, therefore, the most important words are *those that give you trouble.* (Emphasis—Adler's.)[26]

  In other words, if a word appears awkward, unusual, or strange within the context there is a good likelihood it is an important term. This is not foolproof, but if you pay attention to the context of the paragraph, you will have a better chance of picking out the main point.
- Keep a dictionary handy. This will slow the reading pace at first, but if you do not know the words it is difficult to understand the meaning. (See Chapter 4 and the section on subject-matter vocabulary.)
- Don't forget your English training, either. Look for the topic sentence of each paragraph. Let this guide your reading notes. Remember, you can find a topic

sentence in the beginning, middle, or end of a paragraph. (Some authors may not even *write* one; it is *implied.*)

- Don't read the texts of different disciplines in the same manner.[27] For instance, when reading a history text look for cause and effect, important people, impact of events on people, turning points, and hints of bias or prejudice by the author. A science book may be more apt to focus on classifications, experimental steps, hypotheses, and unexplained phenomena. That English novel you have been struggling with is bound to have symbolism, character thresholds, a hero, tragic flaws, and a developing message. And, yes, even math books have their particular characteristics. You may need to know which variables, functions, theorems, and axioms are the building blocks of the chapter. Once you realize that all texts are not created equally, it will be easier to find the main point.

- A word about highlighting: If you choose to highlight or underline in your text, be careful. You want to highlight the major points. Too many students just paint the page yellow. This is useless. Note-taking is more effective because it forces you to encode the material. It forces you to put the material into your own words. If you can do this, you *understand* it.

Post-Read

6. Don't shut the book yet. When you have completed the reading, take five or ten minutes to study the notes you just wrote—*now.* Experts tell us eighty percent of what you just read can be lost within twenty-four hours if you don't review. Organize and reorganize your notes according to categories, theories, trends, or some other categorical grouping. What is the big picture? Can you hook this new knowledge to previously learned material? Can you see any relationships emerging? Believe me, this step will be a blessing in the long run. It keeps you on task, while at the same time prepares you for the next class as well as the coming exam. If you have any confusion about the reading, bring the question(s) to the next class. Maybe, just maybe, you will not have to do any last-minute cramming.

STRATEGY #56

7. Bring your reading outline to class. You are now ready to answer questions, follow the instructor's presentation, and ask your own questions. Since you will be looking at the material for (at least) the second time, you are now studying on the instructor's time. Now, that's efficient!

STRATEGY #57

The "tangential" instructor

Remember that instructor who is always on a tangent, or the one who never seems to have a focus? Well, now you are in a better position to anticipate, follow, and understand his/her presentation. In this manner, you are taking responsibility for your learning. Successful students are active learners.

I have seen students come to class, open their textbook—for the first time—and attempt to follow the lesson and answer questions. If you do this, you might as well raise your hand and tell the instructor, "Mr. Peabody, I didn't do the assignment but your presentation is so dull and predictable I can do it now!"

Not a good way to score points!

8. A word about supplemental sources. If you are still having a difficult time with the textbook, try looking for other sources. For instance, most bookstores sell short versions of American history. Such books concentrate on the major points of historical periods. The same holds true for books in other disciplines. What you are getting with these supplemental books is an outline of major points. This should not be a substitute, but it can help you get through all of the superfluous material.

If you do a book review, use the *Book Review Digest* found in most libraries. This expert analysis of the book will provide you with direction. The same for Cliffs Notes. The point here is *not* to beat the system. It is to help you organize and succeed. Anyway, the good teachers know what's in the Cliffs Notes. Their test questions will definitely go beyond this source.

Guarantees?

There it is. Nothing is sure, but this is an achievable plan. The benefits are many. The notes you develop while reading, for instance, will serve as an excellent guide for your classroom notes. With your reading complete and organized, you are then armed and ready for the teacher's presentation. You can participate; you can be actively learning.

It takes effort—but you did say you wanted better grades. And you will be able to use your precious time more effectively.

Finally, notice that steps 1 through 4 are warm ups. These steps represent a pre-read activity. Step 5 requires the reader to focus and concentrate on the material at hand. The 80/20 principle comes in here.

And the last three steps are important because they will help you develop relationships, which, as we said earlier, are important for comprehension.

Now what?

Now that you've mastered this reading assignment, what can you do with the notes you have?

Bring them to class.

Using reading notes in class serves a variety of purposes. These notes can:

serve as a guide for discussion;

help you answer teacher-posed questions;

remind you to ask clarifying questions;

allow you to focus on the important points the teacher is making. If you are familiar with the material, taking notes will be that much easier to accomplish (remember our last topic?). You will be more prepared to listen and participate actively.

Apply the strategies you've learned to the following passage taken from a business textbook.[28] Review the eight-step plan on pages 74–82. Now, attack the following reading assignment.

Your plan to read the section on Small Businesses will include:

1. What is your purpose? What are you looking for in this reading?
2. How might you "warm up" for this assignment?
3. When initially skimming the passage, what questions have you developed to help you focus?
4. What other clues and guideposts are you using from the assigned text?
5. How will you "chunk" the information for your notes?
6. Once you have finished the passage and have the big picture, how will you reorganize and relate this information? What are the main points?
7. Can you think of any supplemental sources that may help you with this assignment?

WHAT IS SMALL BUSINESS?

How can one recognize a small business? Sales, number of employees, assets, net worth, market share, and relationship to competitors have all been used to make this determination. The official definition from the Small Business Administration says that a small business is a firm that is independently owned and operated, is not dominant in its field, and meets certain size standards for its income or number of employees. Some standards apply only for loan programs, others for procurement, and still others for various special programs. In general, a small business has the following characteristics:

• Independently owned
• Independently operated and managed
• Only a minor player in its industry
• Fewer than 400 employees
• Limited capital resources

Small businesses are more common than one might think. In fact, 95 percent of all enterprises in the United States employ fewer than 50 people each. Further, 20 percent of the companies started last year are one- and two-person operations. Consider that 47,000 consultancies in the United States hire three or fewer people; the number of such firms has doubled in the last 2 years alone. Small companies operate in nearly every industry, including farming, retailing, services, and high technology.

Typical small business ventures

Small businesses compete against some of the world's largest organizations and against a multitude of other small companies. Retailing and service establishments are the most common nonfarming small businesses, and new-technology companies often start as small organizations.

Most farming is still the work of small businesses. The family farm is a classic example of a small business operation that is independently owned and operated, with relatively few employees, but with a substantial amount of unpaid family labor.

General-merchandise giants like Wal-Mart, Kmart, and Sears may be the best known retailing firms, but small, privately owned retail enterprises outnumber them. Small businesses run retail outlets for shoes, jewelry, office supplies and stationery, apparel, flowers, drugs, convenience foods, and thousands of other products.

Other small business ventures include service-oriented industries and individuals such as restaurants, funeral homes, banking establishments, movie theaters, dry cleaners, carpet cleaners, shoe repairers, attorneys, insurance agents, automobile repair shops, public accountants, dentists, and physicians. Small companies often succeed in service industries because they are flexible enough to take on challenges that large service providers overlook. Consider San Diego–based Acucobol, which helps companies to transfer important programs written in the computer language COBOL to newer software. COBOL is an old language in computer terms—it's been around since the early 1960s. Many American firms still have enormous backlogs of vital business applications in COBOL, such as payroll and invoicing programs.

Enter Pamela Coker, who started Acucobol to make these programs compatible with newer computer languages. Coker has succeeded in a market that many software firms have bypassed; she actually has fewer competitors now than when she started the company. "Everybody thinks COBOL's dead," she says cheerfully. "The negative press has provided this hidden, secret market for us." She points out that, in many areas of the world, COBOL remains the dominant language of business computing; 50 percent of Acucobol's revenues come from outside the United States.

Many new-technology firms, those that strive to produce and market scientific innovations, start as small businesses. Many great inventors have launched companies in barns, garages, warehouses, and attics. Small business is often the best (or only) option available to someone seeking to transform a technical idea into a commercial reality.

While most new businesses operate in industries that impose limited capital requirements, some technical firms require substantial capital to get off the ground. Sometimes larger, established corporations provide funding that enables these start-ups to pursue research and develop new products. For instance, several large pharmaceutical companies have formed joint ventures with small biotech firms to identify and market commercial applications of genetic research. SmithKline Beecham invested $125 million in Human Genome Sciences, a Maryland-based start-up that is working to decipher the functions of specific human genes. While Human Genome Sciences has not yet developed any commercial products, its managers plan to patent their discoveries and use the information to develop marketable applications. SmithKline Beecham's investment gives it product rights and a 7 percent stake in future profits.

ADVANTAGES OF A SMALL BUSINESS

Small businesses are not simply smaller versions of large corporations. Their legal forms of organization, market positions, staff capabilities, managerial styles and organization structures, and financial resources generally differ from those of bigger companies. These differences give them some unique advantages.

Innovation

Small firms are often the first to offer new products to the marketplace; Federal Express and Apple Computer are classic success stories. A more recent success is Specialty Silicone Products, a start-up company that makes high-tech rubber products. The firm's best sellers are seals for gas chromatographs, computerized devices used in drug testing and blood analysis. Specialty Silicone makes high-quality stoppers from Teflon-coated silicone that can take up to 150 punctures from hypodermic needles and still block out foreign contaminants that could affect test results. The little company ships $6 million worth of products every year, 17.5 percent of them to overseas markets. Says CEO Daniel Natarelli, "Anybody doing analysis uses these machines—every laboratory, hospital, police lab, and university, even high schools. The world is exploding with gas chromatographs."

Better customer service

A small firm can often operate more flexibly than a large corporation, allowing it to tailor its product line and services to the needs of its customers. As television broadcasts reach all over the globe, for example, more people are demanding specific products. Pooyransh Saini's store in the remote village of Kotputli in northwestern India may measure only 8 feet by 6 feet, but he is the sole retailer in his area to offer the Western brands that are becoming popular with his neighbors. His customers can choose between brand 555, a locally made detergent, and Surf, a detergent made by Unilever subsidiary Hindustan Lever. Notes Saini, "If you don't stock what people see on television, you lose customers."

Lower costs

Small firms can often provide products more cheaply than large firms can. Small firms usually have fewer overhead costs—costs not directly related to providing specific goods and services—and can earn profits on lower prices than large companies can offer.

A typical small business has a lean organization with a small staff and few support personnel. The lower overhead costs due to a smaller permanent staff can provide a distinct advantage to a small business. Such a firm tends to hire outside consultants or specialists, such as attorneys and accountants, only as needed. By contrast, larger organizations often keep such specialists as pemanent staff members. As a rule, all growing organizations add staff personnel faster than line (or operating) personnel.

Consider the Brockton, Massachusetts area, where a growing population of immigrants have come to live from the west African republic of Cape Verde. When businesspeople need a translator to help them communicate with this expanding market, they can call on Chrissy Correia. This 15-year-old girl, who has been confined to a wheelchair since being shot at age 3, started her translation business after attending an entrepreneurship conference at Babson College. Her low overhead—the company is headquartered in her bedroom—allows her to charge less than a large translation firm could. Correia is also starting another venture, Crazy Creations, to sell hand-decorated baskets and watches with an African theme. "I'm taking orders. I hope to build my own business," says Correia. Her family supports her entrepreneurial goals. "They see I'm getting my life together. I'll make something of myself."

Small businesses such as Correia's often have the benefit of unpaid labor. Entrepreneurs themselves are usually willing to work long hours with no overtime or holiday pay. In addition, family members contribute significant unpaid labor as book-keepers, laborers, receptionists, delivery personnel, and the like.

To keep costs as low as possible, many entrepreneurs start their companies in their homes. This can be a good idea or a disaster, depending on the nature of the business and the nature of the entrepreneur. Some lines of work are better adapted to a home setting than others. Table 5.1 lists 10 professions in which a significant number of entrepreneurs earn six-figure annual incomes from their homes.

PROFITABLE HOME-BASED BUSINESSES   TABLE 5.1

BUSINESS ACTIVITY	ESTIMATED ANNUAL INCOME	ESTIMATED START-UP COST (MAXIMUM)
Bill auditing	$50,000–$200,000	$ 7,400
Business broker	Up to $100,000	6,500
Business-plan writer	$24,000–$100,000	10,500
Advertising/marketing copywriter	$20,000–$175,000	6,200
Desktop video producer	$35,000–$150,000	22,000
Executive search	Average $123,000	9,400
Export agent	$60,000–$100,000	10,500
Home inspector	Average $100,000	9,300
Management consultant	Average $110,000	8,800
Professional-practice consultant	$90,000–$187,500	9,800

Business writers recommend the following guidelines for those who want to work at home:

- Love your work. Many people want to work at home because they love being home, not because they are passionate about what they're doing. However, working at home means no boss and no co-workers to get you motivated, so the motivation must stem from the work itself. "The work must be at least a 7 on a scale of your interests ranked from 1 to 10," notes business author Paul Edwards, not "something that makes you bury your head under the covers in the morning and go back to sleep."
- Research the market and the field. Talk to business owners in the field to see if they enjoy working from home. Make sure there's a demand for the business.
- Stay flexible. Sometimes what you want to do isn't necessarily what customers want from you. When Ernest Fine left IBM after 28 years to start his own business, he planned to provide long-term strategic planning help for clients. He changed his focus, however, when he discovered that what customers really wanted was someone to help them solve computer problems quickly.
- Respect your neighborhood. Neighbors may complain, and even force a business owner to move to an office, if a home-based company creates too much traffic or noise in a residential area. "The best businesses to do from home are very silent ones," notes Coralee Kern, executive director of the National Association for the Cottage Industry.

Filling Isolated Niches

The size of a big business excludes it from some markets. High overhead costs force it to set minimum sizes for targets at which to direct competitive efforts. Some large publishers, for example, identify minimum acceptable sales figures that reflect their overhead costs. Editorial and production expenses for a certain type of book may not be justified unless the publisher can sell, say, 7,000 copies. This situation provides substantial opportunities for smaller publishers with lower overhead costs.

In addition, certain types of businesses lend themselves better to smaller firms. Many service businesses illustrate this point. Finally, economic and organizational factors may dictate that an industry consist essentially of small firms. Upscale restaurants are an example.

Clark Childers, a 16-year-old boy who lives in Corpus Christi, Texas, founded a successful business by focusing on a niche market: sailboat owners. While Childers loved sailing, he hated the cover that protected his boat because it was so hard to position. "It was like trying to slip a straw back into its paper covering," he says. So Childers designed a simple nylon cover with an elastic band that fit over the boat as easily as a hairnet, taking only 60 seconds to install. Childers decided to market it. Christened QuikSkins, his cover is manufactured in Mexico and distributed through a Rhode Island dealer. To date, Childers has sold 300 units at $100 a piece, and he is developing other sailing-related products.

Childers' mother helps out during peak periods; one recent evening, they worked together from 5 P.M. to midnight to pack QuikSkins for shipping. "Mom loves this," says Childers. "She considers herself my promotional manager."

DISADVANTAGES OF A SMALL BUSINESS

Small firms also have a variety of disadvantages, including a potential for poor management, a risk of inadequate financing, and goverment regulation. A small firm can be more vulnerable than a large, diversified corporation during a recession, since it probably has fewer resources to cushion a fall. Figure 5.2 shows the survival rate of new businesses in a variety of industries; on average, nearly 62 percent of all businesses dissolve within the first six years of operation. While small business owners can overcome these problems, it is important to think carefully about all of these issues before starting a company.

Poor Management

Poor management is a common reason why small businesses fail. Frequently, people go into business with little, if any, business training. Someone may launch an enterprise based on a great idea for a good or service, assuming that knowledge about business matters will come as the firm operates. Bankruptcy is often the result. Heed a word of caution: If you want to start a business, learn the basics of business first. It is also important to recognize your limitations; few business owners possess the specialized knowledge of an attorney or an accountant, for instance. Successful business owners know when to call on outside professionals for help.

Moreover, small business owners sometimes let their entrepreneurial optimism run wild. Full of excitement about projects and their potential, they may forget about details like paperwork. They may also neglect to "do their homework" before starting the small business. The belief that others will see a product as unique or better than that of the competition should be verified by marketing research. Entrepreneurs should ask themselves whether a market exists for what they want to sell and whether they can convince the public that they offer an advantage over the competition. Published sources, surveys, in-depth interviews, competitive analyses, observation, or a number of other research techniques can provide the answers to those questions.

Economist Kathryn Stafford notes that successful entrepreneurs who work at home tend to use professional practices in their business. These practices include using an answering machine or answering service to handle phone calls when no one is available; hiring an accountant and attorney for specialized advice; borrowing money from a bank, rather than a family member or friend, to finance the business; advertising in the Yellow Pages; and reserving space at home exclusively for business use.

SURVIVAL RATES OF BUSINESSES — FIGURE 5.2

SURVIVAL RATE OF BUSINESS (SHOWN AS %)	YEARS OF SURVIVAL		
	<2	2-4	4-6
Total, All Industries	76.1	47.9	37.8
Construction	77.1	45.6	35.2
Manufacturing	78.7	56.2	46.2
Transportation, Communication, Public Utilities	75.7	46.2	37.0
Retail Trade	75.6	48.1	37.0
Finance, Insurance, Real Estate	74.2	46.2	36.0
Services	75.4	46.5	37.3

Perhaps the most important professional practice is to create a written business plan before starting a business; many entrepreneurs who go into business without one end up regretting it. A later section of this chapter will discuss guidelines for creating an effective business plan.

Inadequate Financing

Inadequate financing is another leading cause of small business problems. Many businesses start with inadequate capital and soon run short of funds. They often lack the resources to survice rough periods or to expand if they are successful. The biggest problem is uneven cash flow; finding funds to pay taxes and employees ranks second.

Most financing for a typical small business comes from the entrepreneur's own resources. Banks provide relatively little funding for small companies. Home-based entrepreneurs may find it especially difficult to qualify for bank loans. "Conventional financing for most home-based businesses is minimal," says Gene Fairbrother, a consultant with the National Association for the Self-Employed.

Entrepreneurs may turn to venture capitalists for funding. **Venture capitalists** are business organizations or groups of private individuals that invest in promising new firms. Sometimes venture capitalists lend money to businesses; other times they become part-owners of new or struggling companies.

The Small Business Administration offers a variety of loan programs for small businesses, primarily through banks. Firms use these loans to finance construction, conversion, or expansion; for purchasing equipment, facilities, machinery, materials, and supplies; and for operating funds.

venture capitalist
Business organization or a group of private individuals that invest in new firms.

Government Regulation

Small business owners complain bitterly of excessive government regulation and red tape. The Small Business Administration estimates that government paperwork costs small firms billions of dollars each year. A larger firm with a substantial staff can usually cope better with the required forms and reports. Many experts within and outside government recognize a need to reduce the paperwork required of small businesses, since they are simply not equipped to handle the burden. Some small firms close down for this reason alone.

TIP! If you will recall, doing homework is not necessarily studying. Completing the homework is the first step. But you need to review, reorganize, and find relationships as you study. If you take the reading notes to class, they will become, automatically, a study aid. The strategy here is simple—as you review the notes in class, you are, in effect, studying on the teacher's time. No more cramming for an exam!

One last strategy on this topic. As a self-assessment, ask yourself if you could intelligently discuss the reading material in class discussion. If you can, congratulate yourself. If you can't, you may wish to review the assignment briefly before you get to class.

STRATEGY #58

Remember that practice makes permanent!

My instructor always falls behind schedule.

Instructors have great intentions. They meticulously plan a unit of study, neatly matching and spacing reading assignments to complement well-thought out lectures. The climax is the unit exam.

Unfortunately, great plans get lost in reality and time constraints of day-to-day classroom activities.

Have you ever had an instructor who painstakingly covered one chapter in three weeks— only to finish the unit with a "big push" to cover four chapters in three days? This introduces an element of stress for everyone concerned, but *you* have to deal with it.

While it's best to read along with lectures (preparing for the lecture prior to coming to class), don't wait to digest ninety pages of new material in a couple of nights. Put yourself on a schedule (see Chapter 3), read, and keep the outlines handy for when the teacher finally reviews material in class.

STRATEGY #59

I've followed the plan, but my reading comprehension is still lousy!

You might find this prescription far from a miracle cure. It may be downright uncomfortable. But so are failed reading quizzes.

Build your vocabulary (part I). This means using a dictionary to clarify meanings. Look up new words, correct misspellings on exams and homework, and become familiar with synonyms and antonyms. A pocket-sized dictionary and thesaurus are two of the most valuable, yet inexpensive books you should have on your desk.

STRATEGY #60

Build your vocabulary (part II). For fifteen minutes in the morning, while you are having breakfast, work on the daily crossword puzzle in the newspaper. This has two benefits: it helps build your vocabulary, and it limbers up your "mental muscles" for the coming academic day.

STRATEGY #61

The reading plan is fine for textbooks—but what about novels?

You have a point. Most novels do not provide the reader with neat headings and subheadings. Chapters might be identified only by a number rather than a descriptive title. Planning the reading attack will be more difficult, but not impossible. It just takes some creativity. Here are some techniques that may work.

STRATEGY #62 Once you have completed reading a chapter, give it your own title. Whatever title you choose, it should answer the question, "What is the essence of this chapter?" Be as creative and descriptive as you can.

STRATEGY #63 Why was the chapter written? Briefly summarize the purpose of the chapter and its connection with the rest of the book. Closely tied to this is a brief summary—what happened and why? Even if you can't identify the plot, this will help point you in the general direction.

STRATEGY #64 Identify any characters introduced, their relationship with other characters, their significance, and their connection to the plot. Did anyone utter a particularly meaningful quote? (You know how English instructors *love* to ask who said what to whom and why.) Some students have found charactergrams beneficial. For those who learn better with pictures and diagrams, the following may be particularly useful:

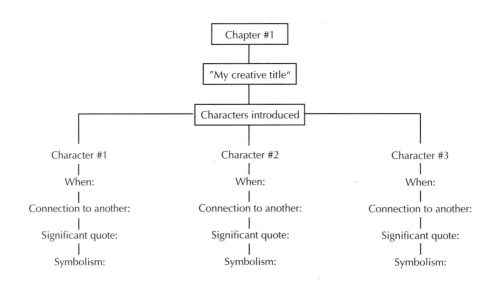

Be sensitive to symbols. Is water being used as a symbol of rebirth, or an old animal synonymous with dying, or autumn representative of old age? Add these to the charactergram as appropriate.

Finally, make a note of what you do *not* understand. Be as specific as possible. Ask a friend and/or the instructor for guidance.

A QUICK REVIEW

This chapter presented efficient reading strategies to improve comprehension. Always know your purpose for reading. Be sure to warm up first by doing a quick skim of the material in front of you. Find the big picture—the main idea. Finally, evaluate *your* reading comprehension. Are you ready to participate in class?

If you follow the tips in this chapter, you are much closer to becoming an active learner—rather than a passive receptacle waiting for the teacher to act on you.

School is more than a place where young people
come to watch old people work!

If we go back to our analogy of taking a trip, you can easily see how all of this ties together. Remember, we're trying to be as efficient as possible.

- You need to know where you are going before you leave.
- You need to map out the most effective way to get there.
- Your notes of the trip will allow for easy and quick review of the trip so you do not have to travel over the same long territory again.
- You need to read actively (your map, road signs). Know your purpose and go after it. If you do not know what to look for, you certainly will get lost!

Specifically, our successful student is able to:

- identify a purpose for reading an assignment
- effectively skim and scan a reading assignment
- succinctly summarize a reading passage in his/her words
- use supplemental sources to complement a reading assignment
- continually build his/her vocabulary

Summary of learning style correlations

TOPIC	AUDITORY	KINESTHETIC	VISUAL
Pre-reading	write or tape-record questions to guide your reading	put questions on flash cards and physically manipulate as you find answers to your questions	write questions; highlight key words
Reading	outline notes	underline and/or highlight; draw charts or timelines	outline notes/draw charts or timelines
Supplemental sources	pre-recorded tapes of texts	videos	pictures; videos
Reading novels	create outline; margin notes	write important information on index cards	flow charts and charactergrams

General comments about your learning environment:

- Your study space should have the appropriate lighting and comfort level.
- Try to read at a time of day when your energy level is at its highest.

CHAPTER 6

THAT SOUNDS GOOD—
BUT I HAVE NO IDEA
WHAT IT MEANS

- Introduction
- Goals
- Time management
- Classroom expectations
- Reading strategies
- ✔ **Writing and research strategies**
- Memory and relationships
- Test preparation
- Summary

1. **Starting it, supporting it, concluding it, evaluating it**
   Your English instructor knows best
   I think my essay is great—too bad my instructor does not share the same view
   Writing decisions
   Look at your T.O.E.S.
   Stating it: Thesis statements
   Supporting it: The body of the essay. The 5 & 5 principle
   What do I do about writer's block?
   Concluding it: The clincher
   The big picture
   Evaluating your work: How do you know if you have written an acceptable essay?

2. **Research and the library**
   Writing a research paper
   Help! I don't know what to write about.
   But how do I prove this opinion? How do I organize my evidence?
   Help! I'm lost in the stacks and I can't get out!
   How do I know what stuff is important?
3. **A quick review**

> *True eloquence consists in saying*
>
> *all that is proper, and nothing more.*
>
> —*François de La Rochefoucauld*

STARTING IT, SUPPORTING IT, CONCLUDING IT, EVALUATING IT

Your English instructor knows best!

Recently, I walked into a colleague's campus office. This English instructor's wall was lined from corner to corner with every conceivable book on writing style, techniques, strategies, and the like.

The point? For the most part, you will receive competent writing instruction from your English department. The purpose of this chapter is not to teach you how to write. Such an endeavor is beyond the scope of this book. My intent is to introduce and reinforce some basic strategies. These techniques will help with homework writing assignments and essay exams (see Chapter 8).

If you'll remember, when we discussed reading strategies, I stressed that you have to know your purpose before you start to read. The purpose helps to guide your approach so that you may effectively and efficiently accomplish the assigned task. The same holds true for writing.

STRATEGY #65 Before writing, you need to know why you are writing. What is it your teacher expects from your efforts?

There are various types and styles of writing. You will, at some point in your classroom career, be asked to create essays that are either descriptive, narrative, comparative, or argumentative. Some essays focus on "how to" do something, while others are more interested in describing cause and effect.

Please keep in mind that this chapter will not cover each style of writing. We will look at basic strategies designed to help you *start* writing. In particular, we will review the basic five-paragraph argumentative/persuasive essay. This is the essay style that attempts to prove a point. Many exam essays are of this nature.

But a word of caution: There is a point at which the five-paragraph format is inappropriate, rigid, and restrictive. Don't get caught in the mindset that you can write only five paragraphs. Some prompts might actually ask you to address four or five points. Your essay can easily be longer than five paragraphs.

Don't put yourself in a writing straitjacket; don't be a slave to a formula. There are, however, some basic rules to get you started.

I think my essay is great—too bad my instructor does not share the same view.

Before you start writing, plan your response. As with any of our topics, always make sure you know what your instructor wants before you start writing. Read the instructions **out loud** (when appropriate). Make sure you **hear** what you are to do. A quick and effective method is to "mark up" the prompt. Develop a series of symbols (underline, circle, and box for instance) to highlight the key tasks in the essay instructions. Let's analyze the following prompt. The tasks (what you are to do) are underlined, the key issues circled, and other important parameters are boxed.

STRATEGY #66

Underline the purpose of the New Colonial System and evaluate its impact on colonial solidarity during the period of 1763–1775.

Once you have accomplished this, a quick outline can develop:

New Colonial System (1763–1775)
    what was it?
    who did it?
    why was it done?
    results on solidarity?
        describe
        my judgment—good, bad? what criteria will I use?

ACTIVITY

Pick an essay prompt from a previous class exam, a current assignment, or one you've developed from your notes. Underline, circle, and box as appropriate. Develop a rough outline.

_____

_____

_____

_____

_____

Writing decisions

There is a simple formula for writing. It is not that difficult. But you have to address certain questions before you start. Do not go into the assignment blindly.

**STRATEGY
#67**

Some of the more basic decisions a writer must make include determinations about:

> topic (for our purposes, I will assume the teacher has assigned a topic—the usual situation on an exam)
>
> an opinion on the topic
>
> supporting evidence for the opinion
>
> the audience for whom the writing is intended (for our purposes, the teacher)
>
> the organization of the paper
>
> who will proofread the essay (besides you)

Most teacher-assigned essays require a string of related paragraphs that explain, analyze, argue, or persuade the reader about a particular topic. Here is an exercise to get your writing juices flowing.

Look at your T.O.E.S

T.O.E.S. is an acronym (see Chapter 7) to help you remember the main components of a basic essay. Your essay must have a <u>T</u>opic, an <u>O</u>pinion, supporting <u>E</u>vidence, and a <u>S</u>ummary. If you ever forget, just look at your T.O.E.S.

Try the following reinforcement activity.

Please write the following:

T   The name of one of your best friends—just the name.

_____

_____

O   State an opinion about that person (Timmy is a very considerate individual).

_____

_____

E   List three facts that support your opinion about this individual.

_____

_____

S   Write a one-sentence summary.

_____

_____

Do the same exercise again. But this time convince someone of something you should be allowed to do.

T: _____

O: _____

_____

E: 1. _____

    2. _____

    3. _____

S: _____

_____

One more time: Organize an answer to a textbook or lecture question.

T: _____

O: _____

_____

E: 1. _____

    2. _____

    3. _____

S: _____

_____

_____

❖❖❖

Stating it: Thesis statements

Do you know what you have just written? This is the beginning of a thesis or main-idea statement. Now I'm sure you have encountered this somewhere along the line in school—but for some reason this relatively simple process is a stumbling block for lots of young scholars. There is nothing mystical about this.

Please read the following clarifying remarks. Then, complete the first four exercises.

WRITING MAIN-IDEA (THESIS) STATEMENTS

Every main-idea statement must contain:

1. The topic
2. Your opinion
3. The direction of your argument (the areas you will use to prove your thesis). Think of this as a **road map** for your reader.

Some hints for writing clear thesis statements:

1. Be sure to address the topic. This sounds simple, but so many students miss this basic point.
2. State only one opinion. Do not try to prove two or more arguments. In other words, **focus on your task.**
3. State an opinion, not just a fact. You will have more success building an argument around an opinion rather than a fact. For example:

Difficult to argue: Ronald Reagan was president. (fact)

Easier to argue: Ronald Reagan was an effective president. (opinion)

4. Provide a brief road map so the reader knows how you plan to develop your opinion. For example:

Lack of clear direction: Ronald Reagan was an effective president.

Direction provided: To prove that Ronald Reagan was an effective president, just look at his record in foreign affairs, health-care reform, and crime control.

Exercise 1: Put a check mark next to the clearly stated thesis statements. Remember to use the criteria established above.

1. Swimming is a sport.
2. Students who continually practice note-taking strategies, time-management strategies, and active reading techniques will become more confident students.
3. This is an effective study skills book.
4. The successful student.
5. I am a successful student because I do all of my homework, listen carefully to instructions, and establish realistic goals.

Exercise 2: Please review and rewrite the poorly written thesis statements of Exercise 1. Use the space below.

_____

_____

_____

_____

_____

_____

_____

_____

Exercise 3: For each of the topics below, please write an opinion. Remember to establish an arguable position. Simply stating "I like my brother" is difficult to argue; it is more a statement of fact than a statement of inference.

1. Study skills
2. Football
3. School

Exercise 4: Now that you have established clear opinions, how will you prove them? That is, what points will you use? Write these revised sentences below.

_____

_____

_____

_____

_____

_____

_____

_____

_____

Although answers may vary, these are some possibilities for the exercises you just completed:

Exercise 1: Put a check mark next to the clearly stated thesis statements. Remember to use the criteria established above.

1. Swimming is a sport.
✓2. Students who continually practice note-taking strategies, time-management strategies, and active reading techniques will become more confident students.
3. This is an effective study skills book.
4. The successful student
✓5. I am a successful student because I do all of my homework, listen carefully to instructions, and establish realistic goals.

Exercise 2: Please review and rewrite the poorly written thesis statements of Exercise 1. Use the space below.

1. Swimming is a sport that requires great endurance. Every muscle is used as the swimmer must constantly propel himself.
3. This is an effective study skills book because it is easy to read, well organized, and provides practical strategies.
4. If a student develops efficient time-management skills, purposeful reading techniques, and realistic goals, she will become a successful student.

Exercise 3: For each of the topics below, please write an opinion. Remember to establish an arguable position. Simply stating "I like my brother" is difficult to argue; it is more a statement of fact than a statement of inference.

1. Study skills: Effective study skills separate the successful from the unsuccessful students.
2. Football: Football is a sport that requires both brain and muscle power.
3. School: School is a necessary training ground for a productive life.

Exercise 4: Now that you have established clear opinions, how will you prove them? That is, what points will you use? Write these revised sentences below.

1. Effective study skills separate the successful from the unsuccessful student by developing responsible habits, attitudes, and academic strategies.
2. The complexity of plays, and the coordination of movement among eleven players, along with the brute strength involved, proves that football is a sport that requires both brain and muscle power.
3. School is a necessary training ground for a productive life as it helps students develop interpersonal relations, communication skills, and vocational abilities.

The above items are *rough* examples to illustrate the components of a thesis statement. As you become more sophisticated in your writing, it will become obvious that a thesis statement need not—and probably should not—be limited to one sentence; it will usually encompass a paragraph. Until you get to that point, your teachers will be thrilled with a complete and logical main-idea statement.

Once you can do the above, work on more extensive thesis statements. Your formula might look like this:

STRATEGY #68   First sentence: Briefly establish the background, or context, for the topic you are addressing.

Second, third, and fourth sentences: Give a broad overview of the points you will use to prove your opinion.*

Fifth sentence: State your opinion. This is the position you will be proving in the body of the essay.*

*You can switch this order; it's really a personal preference—but always check with your instructor.

Another way to accomplish this process is by asking yourself questions. For example,

Topic: My best friend Igor.

(Question: Why is Igor my best friend?)

Opinion: Igor is my best friend because he is one of the most compassionate people I have ever met.

(Question: How do I know Igor is so compassionate?)

Evidence: a. He's always willing to listen.

      b. He's ready to help at a moment's notice.

      c. He never says a mean word.

Summary: Igor's compassion is evident in thought, word, and deed.

Continuing with an example from earlier in the chapter:

T: The New Colonial System

O: The strict enforcement of Britain's New Colonial System brought the colonists closer than ever before as they united against a common enemy.

E: 1. New imperial legislation (Sugar and Stamp Acts)

    2. Colonial meetings to map out strategy (Stamp Act Congress)

    3. Colonial networking (Committees of Correspondence)

S: When England switched from a permissive imperial system to a more stringently enforced program of laws, the colonists became more defiant than ever.

Supporting it: The body of the essay.
The 5 & 5 principle

A very simple rule of thumb is to develop a five-paragraph essay, with each paragraph consisting of at least five sentences. You have already developed the basis for a thesis paragraph. Now you have to support that thesis. Everything that follows in paragraphs two, three, and four must be directly related to the thesis.

STRATEGY #69

Most class essay assignments test your knowledge of material. They are not the origins of the next great American novel. Keep it to the point. All sentences in a paragraph should relate to the topic of the paragraph, and all paragraphs should relate to and support the thesis. Anything else is fluff—that is, beyond-the-scope writing.

STRATEGY #70

Once you have a thesis written, it's time to support your position. There is no substitute for *knowing* the material. The challenge most students face is to organize the data they do have. Why not try clustering?[29]

This technique is great for making sense of the information at your finger tips. On a separate piece of paper, place your main topic in the middle of the page. Now, without stopping to organize anything, write all the subtopics (supporting data) around this topic.

STRATEGY #71

Let's assume you have to write an essay about the challenges faced by the new United States government following the Revolutionary War. This is one way you may wish to organize your thoughts. (Refer to the organizational model introduced on page 57.)

[supporting evidence]   [supporting evidence]

1. Who would rule the **government**?   2. What would replace English
                                            industrial goods?

[main topic]

The new national government had to address many critical issues in 1783.

[supporting evidence]

3. What type of **culture** would the new nation have?

Once you have established these major subtopics, it's time to plug in the facts to support your opinion. From the subtopics, draw lines to supporting facts. You should do this in a matter of minutes. Now, take a moment and evaluate what you have.

---

1. Who would rule the government?   2. What would replace English industrial
                                         goods?

[Facts:]   **[Facts:]**

Articles of Confed were weak   No more mercantilism

Taxing power   Need for $

Raising an army   International markets

Method of picking leaders

[main topic]

Problems the new government had to address in 1783.

3. What type of culture would the new nation have?

[Facts:]

Gender relationships

American style painting

The American language

Once you have completed this exercise, use it as a rough outline for your supporting paragraphs. From here, develop each subtopic into a paragraph. Make sure each paragraph supports the thesis in your introductory paragraph.

What do I do about writer's block?

The best-prepared student will come up empty at times. You've got all your tools but you just cannot get moving. Even a well-tuned car with all the options won't leave the driveway unless the battery is cranking.

When your "writing battery" is drained, you need to jump-start it. But how? Ask yourself the following questions to get moving again.[30]

STRATEGY #72

> Can I relate this to anything else? Are there any groupings or connections?
>
> What are the consequences of this issue?
>
> Is this good/positive or bad/negative? Do others really care about it? How do I feel about it?
>
> Is this an absolute, or are there counter-examples?
>
> How does this fit with a bigger picture?

Concluding it: The clincher

Once you have sufficiently established and supported your thesis, it is time for the clincher—time to close the essay with a powerful thought.

Do not just end your writing. Put your ideas into perspective; state the importance of your opinion. Make sure your main point is not missed. A sophisticated conclusion does not just restate the thesis. It may be an effective idea to reemphasize one or two of your key thesis words, but go further than a simple summary. To arrive at a dynamic conclusion, try asking yourself the following questions:

STRATEGY #73

> Why is this topic/opinion important?
>
> How does my opinion fit into a bigger picture?
>
> Why is this topic significant?

The big picture

We read at the beginning of this chapter that the formula for an effective essay is relatively simple. Below, for the visual learners in the crowd, is a simplistic graphic rendering of the essay flow. Following that is a verbal explanation of the same procedure.

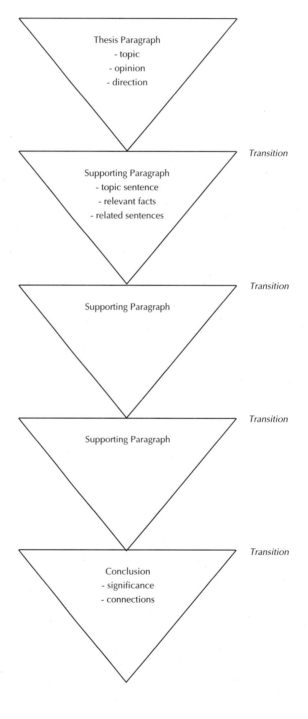

Essay Guidelines: General Information
for Standard Essays

1. Say it. Support it. Conclude it. In other words, make sure you have a clear thesis. Provide arguments or evidence to support your thesis. Tie the essay together at the end.

2. Logically develop your thesis. Stay focused. Do not use a shotgun approach.

3. Content is important—but so is how you present your argument. Pay attention to grammar, diction, syntax, and penmanship. Avoid verbosity. Get to the point. Remember the KISS principle—Keep It Simple Scholar.

4. **Read** the prompt. This sounds simple, but do not overlook it. Carefully digest each word of the prompt. What is the topic? What is the setting? Basically, can you identify the who, what, when, where, and/or why of the item? Before you start writing, you should very carefully read the essay assignment. What is the prompt asking you to accomplish? Underline your tasks so you do not miss them.

STRATEGY #74

This is a partial list of Key Words—words you are most likely to find in essay prompts. You need to **know these words.**

analyze: to divide a topic or issue into its parts; show the relation of one part to another

apply: use your knowledge in a new or different situation

assess: to judge the merits of some issue; evaluate

classify: to put things into categories

compare: to provide similarities, differences, consequences (see *analyze* above)

contrast: to provide differences

criticize: to judge critically

defend: to argue for a particular issue

describe: to explain an event, issue, topic; what are main characteristics

discuss: to explain in detail; go beyond mere description

evaluate: to judge, criticize, establish standards

identify: to show how something is unique or individual

illustrate: to provide examples

interpret: to describe the meaning of an issue

motivations: what caused something to happen

relative importance: to show how two or more factors compare to one another

summarize: to restate briefly

trace: to provide an order or sequence of events

Make sure you understand these words. Do what the teacher calls for. If you are asked to *describe* the **consequences** of World War II, do not *assess* the **motivations** for going to war.

5. **Before** you write the essay, take a moment to plan your response. Jot down a brief outline. Do not go off wildly into a writing frenzy! Take a deep breath, think—and then write. Use the clustering technique here.

6. Although essays come in many shapes and sizes, a traditional format is the five-paragraph essay. Each paragraph usually has five sentences.

A. *Thesis paragraph*: This is the most important part of the essay. It establishes the argument and tone of what is to follow. It also is the first impression you make with your reader. You want to encourage your audience to continue to read. This paragraph should be a mini-essay. Think of it as an inverted triangle (See diagram on page 104).

1. Start by identifying the broad context/setting of the subject at hand.
2. Next, present the arguments (the standards or categories) you will be considering in the essay. These must support your thesis.
3. Finally, state your thesis. What is the main point? <u>What will you be trying to prove in your essay?</u> <u>The thesis should be clear, focused, and specific.</u>

(Depending on style, you can switch 2 and 3.)

When the colonists finally defeated the English in 1783, celebrations took place from Massachusetts to Georgia. Eight years of sacrifice and bloodshed were over. The colonists were independent. Quickly, however, this elation gave way to more serious concerns. The colonists had to build a national government. The nature and shape of this government were still a question. Now that independence had been achieved, the new nation was no longer an official part of the British economic system. The United States had to develop its own economic base. And the newly independent country had to establish its own cultural identity. That is, "What did it mean to be an American?" In effect, although independence had been achieved on the battlefield, political autonomy, economic independence, and a distinct cultural cohesiveness were not foregone conclusions. The leaders of our nation had monumental tasks ahead of them.

<u>Transition sentence leading to next paragraph.</u>

B. *Paragraph 2—Supporting Evidence:* Make sure your paragraph begins with a topic sentence. Although this sentence may introduce the paragraph, it can appear any place. Usually you want it as close to the beginning as possible. Let the teacher know immediately what you are proving in the paragraph. The rest of the sentences should relate to the topic sentence. The entire paragraph should support your thesis. You should include three to five substantial facts that support the thesis. Avoid irrelevant ("fluff") information. Stick to the topic!

During the war, the thirteen states fought as a unit to defeat a common enemy. Maintaining this solidarity, however, was a major challenge for our first central government—The Articles of Confederation.

Following this transition, the student should proceed to support the topic sentence with specific and substantial facts.

<u>Transition</u>

C. *Paragraph 3—Supporting Evidence.* Same format as above, but with a new category or area of argument. The topic sentence should set the tone for the paragraph.

Although a rural-based economic system was in place, the United States had to develop its own industrial base as well as international markets.

Once again, pertinent historical facts would need to follow this introduction.

Transition

D. *Paragraph 4—Supporting Evidence.* Same format as above, but with a new category or area of argument. Again, the topic sentence should set the tone for the paragraph.

While the nation's political and economic foundations were getting a lot of public attention and debate, the cultural identity of America was being more silently shaped. From art to literature to gender relationships, the American society established itself.

Complete the paragraph with relevant support. Be specific with your information.

Transition

E. *Conclusion:* Tie the preceding four paragraphs together. Do not introduce new evidence or a new argument. Do, however, state the significance of your thesis and evidence. Reemphasize one or two key thesis words. That is, what is the connection to a larger body of knowledge? What are the implications of your argument? For short essays, avoid a simple summary. Make sure your reader understands the argument you just presented.

The Revolutionary War established the United States of America as a free and independent nation. It also highlighted the many problems which had to be addressed by the young country. Winning independence was one thing—maintaining it was quite another. A system of government, an economic structure, and a cultural identify needed to be established. Success in these areas was necessary if the nation was to prosper and progress.

Here is a quick summary of the above information:

1. Choose and/or focus on the topic
    know the task you must accomplish
    carefully read all the words
    underline key words
2. Develop a clear thesis statement
    topic
    opinion
    structure of argument
3. Choose your supporting evidence
    make sure your data supports your thesis
    try clustering
    write a key word
    what other words come to mind?
    connect associations

4. Organize your cluster notes
make a brief outline
how to get from the beginning to the end in a logical manner
5. Write
use the strategies you have learned to develop your argument
6. Proofread, revise and submit final product
use the Post-Writing Assessment form (Strategy 75) to evaluate your paper

The length of time you spend on each step will vary according to the actual assignment. An in-class essay will be tackled a bit differently than a long-term project you do for homework. Nonetheless, the steps need to be addressed.

For practice, develop a five-paragraph essay addressing a topic of your choice. Make an argument for your favorite music group, or explain why your parents should let you do something you want to do, or tell your boss why you deserve a raise, or tell the coach why you should start the next game. Pick something and develop a clearly supported argument. You cannot become a better writer unless you practice. The writing skills you develop for the shorter essays you encounter in class will serve you well when it comes time for a lengthier research paper.

❖❖❖

Evaluating your work: How do you know if you have written an acceptable essay?

Use the following checklist to assess the quality of your essay. The successful student does not hand in an assignment just to turn something in. You want it to be reflective of thought and diligence.

Post-Writing Assessment: A Checklist

**STRATEGY
#75**

☐1. Did you correctly interpret the instructions? Did you understand each key word in the prompt?

☐2. Is there a clearly stated thesis (main idea)?

　☐a. Is there a topic?

　☐b. Is there an opinion presented?

　☐c. Did you present a brief "road map" of how you will prove your argument?

☐3. Is all your support relevant to the topic and the opinion? Always ask, "Why is this fact or paragraph important? How does it support my thesis?"

☐4. Is your evidence based on support—or is the essay full of unsubstantiated glittering generalities? For instance, don't say "The government was in lots of trouble." Rather, be more specific and state, "The central government was weak because it lacked the power to tax and control commerce."

☐5. Does the essay follow the sequence you established in your first-paragraph "road map"?

☐6. Have you checked your grammar and sentence structure? Do subjects and verbs agree? What about your syntax and diction?

☐7. Is your writing style and wording appropriate for your audience? That is, is the presentation suitable for the person(s) who will read the essay? As a rule, most school assignments should not use slang. Try not to write like you speak.

☐8. Is the essay neat? (penmanship; errors neatly corrected)

☐9. Have you read your paper aloud? Do this now—and *listen* to your words and sentences. Do they flow? Make sense? (This can be an eye-opening experience!)

☐10. Is your name on the paper?

RESEARCH AND THE LIBRARY

Writing a research paper

Research papers serve various purposes. For one, they allow a student to gain a more in-depth understanding of a particular topic. Some, usually term papers, require the student to *explain* or *describe* a particular topic. Others require the student to develop an actual thesis on an issue and present an argument supporting that particular view. Whatever the thrust of the assignment, you will need to gather source material from experts on your topic.

Once you get over the initial shock of having to prepare a major research paper you'll need to get started. Keep these few basic ideas in mind.

- What are your instructor's directions? Follow them *exactly*. Don't get creative with someone else's instructions. This would include the number of sources required, mechanics of the final product (typed, double-spaced, footnotes or endnotes, bibliographic style—Turabian, MLA, or some other format), and number of pages.

- When is this project due? Circle the date on your long-range planning calendar. Establish a schedule and follow it. Here's a checklist:

Organizing schedule for your paper

☐ Decide on your topic area and your approach to the topic.

Probably the most vital task you will have early in your research is to narrow the focus of your topic. See page 111 for more detailed suggestions

☐ Develop a *temporary* thesis. It's O.K. to revise as you gather data.

☐ What references will you use?

Finding the material in the library. See page 112 for more detailed suggestions.

STRATEGY #76

☐ Go get those references and start taking notes (on note cards).

How do you determine what is important? See page 113 for more detailed suggestions.

☐ Based on your initial research, develop an outline. Do you need to revise your thesis?

☐ More research.

☐ First draft.

☐ Proofread. Get a friend to read it also. Revise.

☐ Second draft.

☐ Proofread and revise.

☐ Final copy completed and submitted *on time*. In fact, get it done early. Remember the Glitch Factor? (See Chapter 3.)

There are two keys to successful completion of your paper:

- focusing on your topic/thesis and
- managing your time. Remember, the assignment is not going to go away. You've got to do it. So make it easy on yourself and break all of the tasks into bite-sized, manageable chunks.

Help! I don't know what to write about.

In most instances, the instructor will give you a broad topic about which to write. Your immediate task will be to narrow the focus of your research. A typical, and understandable, problem most students have is choosing a subject that is far too broad.

STRATEGY #77   If your English instructor assigned a seven-to ten-page paper on the general topic of nineteenth-century writers, what would you do? (Panic is *not* an option.) Well, your first task would be to narrow the topic. What about nineteenth-century writers would you research? Remember, it is a brief paper. (Yes, ten pages is brief.) So writing about the major themes of all European and American writers is ambitious.

ACTIVITY

Brainstorm this topic. Each time you come up with a topic, ask yourself, "Can I narrow this any further? Is this too broad? Can I find enough information on the topic? Will I have too much information with which to work?" Jot your thoughts below.

_____

_____

_____

_____

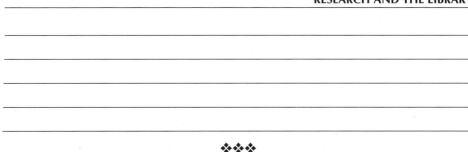

❖❖❖

Maybe you decided to write on nineteenth-century *American* writers. Good start, but this is still too broad. How about writers of the late nineteenth century? Well, that's better but still needs more focus. After all, do you really want to write about *every* late nineteenth-century American writer? By process of elimination you get to concentrating on one writer—Mark Twain. Why did you pick Twain? It should be because he is of interest to you. (When at all possible, pick a topic that will be exciting to you. You have to live with it.)

But wait. Before you go running off in search of books on Huck Finn's creator, you have a bit more work to do. What about Twain are you going to research? His childhood? Early writing influences? Literary successes? Failures? Critics? In other words, you might wish to limit your research to one aspect of his career.

Once you have sufficiently narrowed the topic—the literary style of *Huckleberry Finn,* for example—determine what you will prove. This becomes your central reason for writing. It provides reason for your research and writing. Start with a question: Why has *Huckleberry Finn* been a literary success? Answer the question: "*Huckleberry Finn* has been critically acclaimed because it was written in an idiomatic style that *showed*, rather than merely *described*, what life on the Mississippi was like." This is the thesis you will need to prove in your paper.

But how do I prove this opinion? How do I organize my evidence?

When confronted with a vast array of material, one can be easily overwhelmed. Try the following strategy once you have narrowed your topic and identified your thesis.[31]

Establish a separate list for each of the following: people, events, issues, quotes, places. For the "people" list, jot the names of the critics and experts who support your thesis. Is there an event that supports your thesis? List any with a clear connection to the thesis. How about pertinent issues? Do the same with the remaining lists. Quotes can add punch to your paper. A well-phrased quote about your topic can add the weight of an expert. A word of caution: When used, quotes should be short and sparing. Remember the purpose of the paper is to get *your* thoughts on paper. You are not being asked to write a string of quotations. Be careful in this area. Finally, would a reference to a particular place (e.g., a geographic location) be of help to your argument? If so, include it.   **STRATEGY #78**

A common misconception is that you should be able to sit down and pick a narrowly focused subject with little or no effort. If you have ever grappled with this task, you know it is not that simple. To come up with a reasonable topic you must do some initial   **STRATEGY #79** research. Before you can engage in narrowing a topic you have to know something about it. Start by looking at your class notes, class textbooks (table of contents and bibliography), magazines, general and subject-specific encyclopedias, and related monographs. Take some cursory notes. Develop a "flavor" of the topic. More than likely you will need to make a trip to that formidable building on campus—the library.

So grab your pen, note cards, and coins for the duplicating machine, and head out the door now.

Help! I'm lost in the stacks and I can't get out!

It is not my intent to provide an exhaustive review of how to use the library. There are excellent courses and books[32] already available on the topic. Your instructors can direct you to appropriate sources.

I want *briefly* to mention some of the basics to help with your library search. Keep in mind that each library can have its own nuances. I suggest a library tour to familiarize you with the workings of the facility you will be using. I have never met a librarian unwilling to help a student.

TIP! In fact, get to know the reference librarian as soon as you can. This individual can save you a lot of wasted steps and worry. The librarian will not, and should not, do your research, but will share hands-on knowledge of sources of particular help in your field.

TIP! Every school library will have a catalog of holdings. This is a listing of books and other resources in the library. Think of this as the table of contents for your library. It is your guide to volumes of information. Since card catalogs are being replaced more and more by on-line computer catalogs, I will give some hints on how to use the electronic catalogs.

The catalog allows you to search your topic by author, title, subject or keyword search. A typical opening screen[33] might show something like:

a = author

t = title

s = subject

tj = periodical title

k = keyword search

At this point, type in your choice. You could type

a = twain, mark

Or

t = huckleberry finn

Or

s = 19th century writers

Or

k = twain and criticism

If there is a match in the catalog, the next screen will present any number of choices on the subject you entered on the previous screen. Follow the instructions at the bottom of the screen. Generally, if you type the number beside one of the items on the screen you will see an expanded view of the holding on the screen.

This and following screens usually present the following information:

Author's name

Title of work

Publication information

Physical description of the book (number of pages, illustrations, index)

International Standard Book Number (ISBN)

General subjects to which this book applies (can be of help in locating other material on your topic)

Call number (needed to locate the book on the library shelf/stack)

Status (is the book checked out or on the shelf?)

Follow command choices at the bottom of the screen to move forward or backward among the catalog choices. With just a little practice, you will be able to navigate and access this valuable information quickly from the computer terminal.

STRATEGY #80

With command of the electronic card catalog, you will be able to access other forms of information, electronic or otherwise, more readily. You might wish to look at subject-specific indexes like *American Writers* or *Contemporary Literary Criticism.* Sources such as ERIC (Educational Resource Information Center) will provide a wide range of articles on topics in the educational field. This source, whether used in electronic form or in the older bound-book format, will provide abstracts of articles. Other indexes will provide synoptic views of longer articles. As a researcher, you'll get a quick feel for the source from the abstract and know whether or not it is of use to your particular project.

If your library does not have the electronic card catalog mentioned above, use the bound-book version of the *Readers' Guide to Periodical Literature* to find magazine and journal articles of interest. Newspapers like the *New York Times* also have their own indexes.

There is a wealth of information in the library—but it will do you no good if it remains on the shelves. Research is like putting together a puzzle. You have to patiently search for the correct pieces. Once found, you must know what to do with the information.

How do I know what stuff is important?

STRATEGY #81

Once you have narrowly defined your topic and started to take notes from your source material, the answer to this question will become more readily apparent. Earlier in the chapter, you read the suggestion to ask yourself how each paragraph connects to your thesis. Apply this same principle to your term paper. If you wish to prove that Twain's style was the reason for his success, then you should focus on commentary about his literary skills. Why not see what the experts in the field have to say about the subject? An excellent source is the *Book Review Digest*. The *Digest* provides excerpts from full-length book reviews, complete with analysis and bibliographic citations to find the original review. Other literary digests or indexes will also help you see the nexus of the topic.

A QUICK REVIEW

This chapter presented basic strategies for clear essay writing and basic tips for surviving a research paper.

There are, really, only three ways to become a better writer—practice, practice, and more practice. More specifically, the proficient writer:

- knows the purpose of the writing assignment
- takes time to plan an appropriate response
- establishes an opinion that relates to the topic
- provides evidence that supports the opinion
- does not give up if he/she encounters writer's block
- takes time to evaluate his/her work
- has an organized schedule to complete research papers
- effectively narrows the focus of a research topic to a workable proposition[34]
- is familiar with library resources (print, electronic and human)

Good luck and happy writing.

Some correlations with your learning style

TOPIC	AUDITORY	KINESTHETIC	VISUAL
Analyzing the prompt	physically mark up the prompt; orally dissect the prompt	physically mark up the prompt	physically mark up the prompt
Organizing a paper/essay	pen and paper for a traditional outline; use a tape recorder	when composing your ideas try walking around your room as you think; pen and index cards (for later manipulation)	pen and paper outline; try to "see" the outline of material as it is developing in your mind's eye; use chunking and cluster notes

TOPIC	AUDITORY	KINESTHETIC	VISUAL
Writer's block	turn on a tape recorder and say what comes to mind—a form of stream of consciousness; brainstorm with a buddy	move about; manipulate index cards; cut and paste	stream of consciousness writing; brainstorm with a buddy
The library	read all appropriate handouts; get a supplemental book on using the library	physically tour the facility; manipulate the electronic catalogs	practice with electronic catalogs

General comments about your learning environment:
- Make sure your personal study space is appropriate.
- Are you writing at a time of day when your energies are highest?

CHAPTER 7

WHATSHISNAME SCHEDULED A WHATCHAMACALLIT FOR WHEN?

- Introduction
- Goals
- Time management
- Classroom expectations
- Reading strategies
- Writing and research strategies
- ✔ Memory and relationships
- Test preparation
- Summary

1. **Why do we forget?**
   Selective forgetting
   Why do you forget—and what can you do about it?
   Memory blocks
   The brain's attic
   Retrieval failure
   Memory ≠ understanding
   Memory = the foundation
2. **It's a matter of focusing energies**
   Desire
   Active listening = improved memory
   Strategies for retrieval
   Mental pictures
   Names
   Mnemonics
   Practice
3. **A quick review**

A retentive memory is a good thing,
but the ability to forget is the
true token of greatness.

—*Elbert Hubbard*

Many a man fails to become a thinker
only because his memory is too good.

—*Nietzche*

WHY DO WE FORGET?

Selective forgetting[35]

The quotes at the beginning of this chapter might sound confusing; they seem out of place. Can a good memory actually have a downside? Read on.

STRATEGY #82

You come in contact with a mind-boggling amount of data each day of your life. Your mind already performs a function that successful students know how to conduct—*selective forgetting*. In their book, *Rapid Memory in 7 Days,* Joan Minninger and Eleanor Dugan succinctly state,

> Bright people remember less than average people because they drop out all the small stuff. They can focus their energy on important things instead of trivia.

In order to cope with the vast quantities of information vying for your attention, you choose to focus on only those things you wish. You must have a desire to retain information. No desire—no understanding—no memory!

You will need to develop observational and listening skills. That requires discipline and concentration.

Finally, memory is the process of storing and finding information in the brain. You have to develop an efficient system for retrieving that information. If you have been following the organizational strategies in this book, you are well on your way to establishing effective recall strategies.

Let's start with a little demonstration. Without looking, picture the area to the left of where you are sitting. Describe what you see. Be specific. If there is a bookshelf, don't just say there are books on the shelf. In what order do they appear? What are the topics? What color are the books? Hardcover or soft? Look to your right (mentally again). What kind of furniture is there? Colors? Fabrics? Designs? Length and width?

Think of the last meal you ate with someone. Who was at the table with you? Exactly where did these people sit? What did the people have on? Colors? Styles? Leather, cotton, knit, suede? Socks? Canvas shoes or no shoes?

There are a couple of points to be made here—from which strategies will emerge.

Why do you forget—and what can you do about it?

Forgetting is the failure of a previously *learned* behavior to appear. If you haven't learned it, you cannot possibly forget it.

We forget for a variety of reasons:

1. We fail to use what we have learned.

and/or

2. The reward we received for learning is no longer present.

and/or

3. A previously learned behavior interferes with a newly learned behavior.

and/or

4. A newly learned behavior interferes with a previously learned behavior.

and/or

5. The situation in which the new behavior must occur is different from the one in which the behavior was learned.

Let's develop this list a little further.

Memory blocks

It has happened to all of us at one time or another. We know the material, but we freeze up on the exam or during the presentation. Why?

Emotional memory blocks. Some of us are afraid to challenge ourselves. Whether it is a fear of failure or the memory of some distressing prior experience, we cannot (will not?) perform.

Physical memory blocks. You pulled the proverbial all-nighter. You have reviewed everything that the instructor possibly could ask. You get to the class—and everything is a jumbled mess. You are so tired you cannot think straight. Or you ate too much, or too little, right before an exam. So much for your hours of studying. Concentration is difficult to come by.

Mechanical blocks. You have put a lot of time into your studies, but you can't seem to pull up the data during the exam. This is usually an indication of some retrieval difficulty. The filing cabinet in your brain holds all the information; however, you have just thrown the information into the drawers without labeling. Now you can't find it.

The brain's attic

In very simple terms, you have a short-term and a long-term memory. The short-term can last anywhere from thirty seconds to a couple of days. If the information is not used, it is virtually lost to you. (Some research indicates, however, that it is still <u>in</u> the brain.[36])

The long-term memory consists of those items that have not been "lost." For whatever reason—practice, concentration, desire—you have retained this data.

"But," you reasonably may ask, "why do I still forget things when it comes to test time? I've practiced. I've got desire. But my test grades don't reflect this!"

Retrieval failure

One point we've been repeating is your need for desire. Let me add something to this equation.

desire + effective retrieval strategies = memory

Sounds rather simplistic, doesn't it? But there are a number of obstacles to overcome before you can achieve a more uninhibited retrieval.

Poor labeling. The better your filing system, the better your ability to find the data for which you are looking. Think of your brain as a filing cabinet. Organize the cabinet. Label the drawers, the files, and the folders. When you learn a new piece of information, place it in the proper file folder. Now you know where it is—and you will be able to pull it up when you need it. What would happen if you just threw pieces of paper into the file drawer without any order whatsoever? It is obvious that you would have a difficult time finding material.

Yet this is what a lot of us do with vital information. Just as you would store valuables carefully, do the same with the facts, concepts, and generalizations with which you come into contact. Remember the suggestion to review your notes nightly? The 3 Rs will help you file. Developing connections is the best way to fight against improper filing.

Disuse. Just like your muscles, if you do not use information, you will, more than likely, lose it. Ever have difficulty remembering some course material after a prolonged vacation from school? The reason is simple: you have not used the information. Once you start practicing it again, the process usually returns (assuming you have labeled it correctly).

Extinction. Our schools, are based on a series of rewards. These incentives vary but range from smily faces to grades to awards for a high GPA. Many of us have been conditioned by these extrinsic rewards—that is, those given to us by someone else. The grade, for instance, becomes the overriding reason for performance. Once the reward (grade) is removed, the incentive to continue to work with the material is removed. No reward—no effort—no retention.

Response competition. Visualize this scenario: You have studied for a science exam. Science is the last class of your school day. Before you get to this exam, you have your English, history, math, language, and drama classes. Each subject introduces you to more and more data. Your brain feels as if it is going to burst! Welcome to the world of competing information. If you have not developed a sound retrieval system, frustration is about to set in.

Situational variation. Let's just call this stage fright. You have practiced that guitar lead for months. You never missed a lick. The first time you perform it in public—you guessed it—you fall flat on your face. Or you never flubbed a line during drama rehearsal. Opening night has arrived—and you can't remember your name! Why? The situation, the venue, has changed. You practiced in one environment, but must perform in quite a different situation.

Memory ≠ understanding

Before we move into specific strategies, let's set the record straight on one issue: While an effective memory may be impressive, and it may even help you get by on tests, it does not indicate that you understand the material. In fact, a good memory might end up being one of your (unknown) weaknesses. Sound like a contradiction? Read on.

I am a mechanical klutz. If I had to, I could memorize the parts of a carburetor, but don't ask me to explain their operation. I'm lost. Similarly, I spent many hours in school memorizing lists of vocabulary and spelling words. My exams and quizzes had high scores. But in reality, I never learned the important rules that guide spelling exceptions. This has been a headache in later years as I have had to learn basic spelling rules I should have understood back in elementary school.

The problem: I was too interested in receiving a great grade—the extrinsic motivator. I needed to develop intrinsic rewards—and learn the basic relationships.

 True learning will, and should, cause some frustration. After all, learning indicates a change in behavior. Learning to accommodate new methods and information can be disconcerting to some of us. So, too, with memory strategies. As you review the ideas in the next section, keep two points in mind.

First, since you are not used to them, they will seem awkward at first. Don't give up for that reason alone.

Second, not every technique is for you. Pick and choose—but find something that works for you.

Memory = the foundation

Before you can truly understand material, you need to develop your ability to retain and retrieve information. Once you have established this foundation, understanding the material—in the classroom, in your job, in your hobby—will be close at hand.

desire + efficient filing = understanding

IT'S A MATTER OF FOCUSING ENERGIES

Have you ever been introduced to someone, only to forget his/her name within two minutes? It can be embarrassing. How about dates and numbers? Or your reading assignment (remember Chapter 5)? What's a person to do?

Desire

Most people forget because they *choose not to remember*. It really is that straightforward. Concentration is the name of the game. Listening, for instance, is an activity that requires focus. The task is not to *hear,* but to *listen.*

Active listening = improved memory

Here are a few strategies to help you remember more of what you hear.

- *Focus.* You need to pay attention to the speaker, whether he is your boss, teacher, friend, or parent. I am always amazed by people who *choose* not to concentrate and then complain because they cannot remember a thing! Practice courtesy and you will retain more. Pay attention to the speaker. Put aside other distractions. Focus on the words and meanings.

- *Find relevance.* Face it: not every teacher is going to be a living, breathing dynamo. Find something in the presentation and focus on it. Find a relationship to something you already know.

- *Listen with your ears—not your mouth.* Too many people are busy mentally phrasing their response while the speaker is still speaking. You cannot understand the speaker if you are just waiting to jump in and give your opinion. If you "listen" in this manner, you are creating your own distraction.

- *Participate.* Once the speaker has finished, rephrase what was said. If you can explain in your own words what has just been presented, you will have a better chance of retention. By paraphrasing you are, in effect, rehearsing the new material. Practice leads to understanding.

- *Ask questions.* This is part of the class participation strategy also. Ask for clarification, relationships, or the significance of the topic at hand. Not only are you drilling the information, but you're doing it in the context of the big picture of the presentation. This will help in the development of memory hooks (more below).

- *Offer another explanation or another application.* This is a particularly effective strategy in discussion or seminar-style classes. As you process the new information, try to present another side of the issue. This does not, and really should not, be done in a combative manner. Rather, attempt to understand other aspects. This allows for analysis, and consequently, better understanding.

The key to the above steps is the desire to want to understand. By becoming actively involved, you will be more apt to retain the information.

Strategies for retrieval

STRATEGY #83   It should be obvious that each of this book's topics neatly tie into one another. For instance, if your retrieval problem stems from poor labeling (remember the file cabinet?), review the reading strategies presented in Chapter 5. Skimming, scanning, questioning, outlining, and anticipating are all devised to make information processing more efficient. The more you review (study) the more likely you will be able to retain and retrieve.

"What about my class notes?" you may ask. "I can't make any sense of these scribbles." There are a couple of techniques you can employ here.

STRATEGY #84   First, review the link between Chapters 4 and 5—the classroom experience and reading strategies. Ask yourself, "What are the connections between my homework reading and the class presentations?" With a little practice you will be able to pick these out easily. Once you establish these relationships, you will have an increased ability to retain, understand, and retrieve. You see, this moves beyond sheer memory. The material starts to take on a life of its own. It makes sense.

The Data Retrieval Chart (DRC). Another technique students find particularly helpful is the Data Retrieval Chart—an organizational model long used in education. Its abbreviated format allows for the assimilation of vast quantities of data in an efficient manner. It is an excellent tool for establishing relationships. Not only can you use this to review your notes, but it is a handy outline for organizing your reading assignments.

STRATEGY #85

I have used the following examples with high school and college students. This particular model was developed for students studying the American War for Independence.

THE NEW COLONIAL SYSTEM

PRIME MINISTER	BRITISH ACTION	COLONIAL RESPONSE
Grenville		
Rockingham		
Townshend (Pitt)		
North		

This DRC was used to introduce college freshmen to a unit on the Middle Ages.

HEIRS OF THE ROMAN EMPIRE

Introduction: The Middle Ages is the term used for the (approximately) 900 year period from the political demise of Rome (5th century) to the beginnings of Modern Times (approximately 14th to 15th century). The Early Middle Ages is referred to by some historians as the Dark Ages (5th century to 10th century), characterized by general disorder and decline and lack of appropriate administrative machinery. The Later Middle Ages (11th century to 14th/15th century) was a period of more advancement. This period of history generally refers to the western part of the European continent.

	Byzantine Empire	Islamic Empire	Germanic Kingdoms (Early)	Germanic Kingdoms (Late)
Administration				
Contributions				
Events of Significance				
Challenges				

This chart helped a college class compare and contrast the interaction of various minority groups in the United States.

MINORITY STATUS IN THE UNITED STATES

Minority groups have responded in different ways to dominant group reactions. Use this chart to organize your thoughts and analyze the evolution of dominant-minority interaction in the United States of America.

	AFRICAN AMERICANS	HISPANICS	ASIANS	NATIVE AMERICANS
How was minority status achieved?				
Structural factors that have affected the group				
Stereotypes				
Discrimination (examples)				
Adjustment patterns (e.g., assimilation)				
Primary issues relating to the group				
Relative deprivation? (yes/no/evidence)				

	AFRICAN AMERICANS	HISPANICS	ASIANS	NATIVE AMERICANS
What would the dominant group like to say to the minority group?				
What would the minority group like to say to the dominant group?				
What does the future hold?				
Your recommendations				

A student organized a reading assignment with the following.

OF MICE AND MEN

John Steinbeck introduces a variety of characters in this classic novel. Use this chart to analyze the significance of each character to the overall story line.

CHARACTER	WHEN INTRODUCED	SYMBOLISM	SIGNIFICANCE
George			
Lennie			
Slim			
Candy			
Crooks			
Carlson			
Curley			
Curley's wife			
Old dog			

As you can see, the data retrieval chart can be used to compare authors, scientific findings, historical developments, artistic relationships, and the like. Each cell allows for easy comparison to another cell. Relationships, which are vital to improving your memory, are easily established.

Don't wait for the teacher to provide a DRC. Make up your own when reviewing and reorganizing your notes. This is a great one-page study guide—efficient, effective, and practical.

Pause for a moment and read the following excerpt from an introductory text on sociology.[37] Once you have completed reading the section on Theories of Stratification, construct and fill in a data retrieval chart. Compare your product with the version in Appendix C. (Additional practice: Why not employ the reading strategies you mastered in Chapter 5 of this book to complete this short section review? Isn't it amazing how all this fits together?)

THEORIES OF STRATIFICATION

Conflict Theories

As mentioned earlier, Marx's theory of stratification asserts that capitalist societies are divided into two opposing classes, wage workers and capitalists, and that conflict between these two classes will eventually lead to revolutions that will establish classless socialist societies. However, Marx's prediction was not borne out in any society that attempted to implement his ideas on a large scale. Deny it as they might, all of those societies developed well-defined systems of social stratification (Djilas, 1982; Parkin, 1971; Szelenyi, 1983). Each had an elite of high party officials; an upper stratum of higher professionals, scientists, managers of economic enterprises, local party officials, and high police officials; a middle level of well-educated technical workers and lower professionals; a proletariat of industrial and clerical workers and military personnel; and a bottom layer of people who were disabled, criminals, or political outcasts.

No persuasive evidence shows that class conflict is heightening the division between workers and owners of capital in capitalist societies. Conflict does exist, but the industrial working class is shrinking and the new occupational groups do not always share the concerns of the industrial workers. Moreover, reforms of capitalist institutions have greatly improved the worker's situation, thereby reducing the likelihood that the revolution predicted by Marx will occur.

Modern conflict theorists agree with Marx's claim that class conflict is a primary cause of social change, but they frequently debate both the nature of the class structure and the forms taken by class conflict. Thus Erik Olin Wright (1979) notes that Marxian theorists agree that workers who are directly engaged in the production of goods are part of the working class. However. "there is no such agreement about any other category of wage-earners. Some Marxists have argued that only productive manual workers should be considered part of the proletariat. Others have argued that the working class includes low-level, routinized white-collar workers as well. Still others have argued that virtually all wage-laborers should be considered part of the working class."

This disagreement stems, of course, from the fact that there is far greater diversity within all the classes of modern societies than Marx or his contemporaries imagined there would be. In addition to the bourgeoisie (the owners of large amounts of capital) and the petit bourgeoisie (the owners of small firms and stores), there is a constantly growing professional class, a class of top managers and engineers, another class of lower-level managers, and a class of employees with special skills (e.g., computer specialists, nurses and other medical personnel, and operating engineers). Perhaps many of these people should think of themselves as part of the working class, but they normally do not because they are earning enough to enable them to live in middle-class communities.

Some conflict theorists focus on other aspects of social stratification besides class conflict. Melvin Tumin (1967), for example, pointed out that stratification systems "limit the possibility of discovery of the full range of talent available in a society;" that they create unfavorable self-images that further limit the expression of people's creative potential; and that they "function to encourage hostility, suspicion, and distrust among the various segments of a society." Problems like wasted talent and poor self-image are among what Richard Sennett and Jonathan Cobb (1972) term "the hidden injuries of class," meaning the ways in which a childhood of poverty or economic insecurity can leave its mark on people even after they have risen out of the lower classes. In the next chapter we look more specifically at social stratification in the United States and examine its consequences in human terms.

The Functionalist View

The functionalist view of stratification was originally stated by Talcott Parsons (1937, 1940) and Kingsley Davis and Wilbert Moore (1945). This theory holds that social classes emerge because an unequal distribution of rewards is essential in complex societies. Such societies need to reward talented people and channel them into roles that require advanced training, personal sacrifice, and extreme stress. Thus the unequal distribution of rewards, which allows some people to accumulate wealth and deprives others of that chance, is necessary if the society is to match the most talented individuals with the most challenging positions.

The research of sociologists in the former Soviet Union often provided support for the functionalist idea that extreme "leveling" will deprive people of the motivation to achieve more than a minimum of skills. On the basis of extensive surveys of workers in Russia and other former Soviet republics, sociologist Tatyana Zaslavskaya (quoted in Aganbegyan, 1989) argues that unless there are incentives in the form of high wages and other advantages (such as better housing in areas where good housing is in short supply), engineers and scientists will resent their situation and will not work hard. In the United States the same arguments are used to justify higher salaries for doctors, lawyers, and other professionals. Too much equality, it is said, reduces the incentive to master difficult skills, and as a result the entire society may suffer from a lack of professional expertise.

Critics of the functionalist view of inequality and stratification point to many situations in which people in positions of power or leadership receive what appear to be excessive benefits. In the early 1990s, during the most prolonged economic recession the United States had experienced since the Great Depression of the 1930s, the multimillion-dollar salaries of many corporate executives were frequently criticized in business magazines and news analyses. For example, Roberto Goizueta, chief executive officer of the Coca-Cola Company, was criticized for taking home more than $10 million in 1991. Many other executives were earning equally high salaries even when their companies were not doing as well as they might in international competition. With the annual pay of top Japanese executives often running five to ten times less than that of their American counterparts, it became difficult for the American corporate elite to argue that these enormous rates of executive compensation are "functional."

From the point of view of those who are critical of social inequality, these large sums paid to a few people seem wrong, especially when so many others are struggling just to survive. Indeed, the heads of large corporations in the United States often earn more than fifty times as much as the average employee of those corporations. Is such great disparity "functional" when it produces enormous gaps between the very rich and the working classes? Functionalist theory claims that it is, for in a capitalist system of free enterprise top executives will seek the firms that are most willing to reward them for their talents. Those firms will benefit, and so will their workers.

The Interactionist Perspective

Conflict theory explains stratification primarily in economic terms. So does functionalist theory. Both trace the existence of certain classes to the central position of occupation, income, and wealth in modern life. But neither goes very far toward explaining the prestige stratification that occurs within social classes. Among the very rich in America, for example, people who have stables on their property tend to look down on people with somewhat smaller lots on which there is only a swimming pool. And rich families who own sailing yachts look down on equally rich people who own expensive but noisy power boats. The point is that within economic classes people form status groups whose prestige or honor is measured not according to what they produce or how much wealth they own but according to what they buy and what they communicate about themselves through their purchases. Designer jeans and BMW cars are symbols of membership in the youthful upper class. Four-wheel-drive vehicles equipped with gun racks and fishing rods are symbols of the rugged and successful middle- or working-class male. Dress styles that minic those shown on *Miami Vice* are symbols of urbane professionalism; tweed suits and silk blouses are signs that a woman is a member of the "country club set." All of these symbols of prestige and group membership change as groups with less prestige mimic them, spurring a search for new and less "common" signs of belonging (Dowd, 1985).

Our tendency to divide ourselves up into social categories and then assert claims of greater perstige for one group or another is of major significance in our lives. The interactionist perspective on stratification therefore may not be very useful in explaining the emergence of economic classes, but it is essential to understanding the benaviors of the status groups that form within a given class. Those behaviors, in turn, often define or reinforce or challenge class divisions. The stratification system, in this view, is not a fixed system but is created over and over again through the everyday behaviors of millions of people.

Conclusion

"The first lesson of modern sociology," wrote C. Wright Mills in his study of white-collar workers, "is that the individual cannot understand his own experience or gauge his own fate without locating himself within the trends of his epoch and the life-chances of all the individuals of his social layer" (1951). In this chapter we have examined the concepts needed to understand how the phenomenon of "social layering" or stratification arises, how it is related to the means of existence, and how it has changed as human societies have evolved from simpler agrarian forms of production into more complex industrial and even postindustrial societies.

This introduction to social stratification and how it affects life chances has not said much about the class structure of North American society. That is the goal of the next chapter, in which we look in more detail at stratification by wealth, power, and prestige in our own society and compare it with stratification in other societies. Throughout this book, however, we have reason to cite the power of social inequalities, especially inequalities of wealth and power, in shaping people's lives. Few issues are as central to explanations of social change and stability. As we saw at the begining of the chapter, the question of why efforts to build a classless society failed in the former Soviet Union will be with us for decades. The Visual Sociology essay in this chapter shows that despite the failures of the Russian Revolution, impoverished people in other parts of the world still dream of a revolution that will bring them and their children a greater share of the wealth of their societies. And the next chapter shows that struggles to reduce poverty and inequality account for much of the social change occurring in our own nation.

Mental pictures

We have a tendency to think in pictures. We consciously try to put thoughts into images and then cluster these images into relationships. Clustering is a strategy we used with our writing to gather supporting evidence for a thesis. Employ the same technique here—just do it with mental pictures.

STRATEGY #86

For instance, refer to the first DRC on The New Colonial System. Visualize the British in their red coats. See the Boston Tea Party in your mind. Imagine the first shots fired at Lexington and Concord. This sort of creativity uses much more of the brain than if you just attempted to memorize the words without a clear conception of what was actually transpiring. (For a more detailed explanation of this technique, I recommend Kevin Trudeau's *Mega Memory*[38].)

Names

Remembering names does not have to be difficult. One memory expert performed a fascinating exercise for national TV audiences. He went into the studio audience and in a relatively short period of time remembered hundreds of strangers' names.

I'm not proposing anything so dramatic. But a few simple techniques will avoid embarrassment while at the same time impressing people.

- *Decide you want to remember the name.* Make a conscious effort. Say to yourself, "I want to remember this person's name."
- *Listen and repeat.* Carefully listen to the name of the individual. Repeat it. Ask for a spelling of the name. Use the name immediately. An exchange might go something like this:

"Steve, I would like for you to meet my friend Iggie."

"Iggie, I'm pleased to meet you. You know, Iggie is an unusual name. I remember a rock group back in the seventies called Iggie and the Stooges. That wasn't you by chance? Well, it was nice meeting you, Iggie. I look forward to talking with you later."

In about fifteen seconds the new name was used five times. Practice makes permanent.

- *Look at the face.* Lock the name to the face.
- *Notice physical features.* Does this person have any unique features? Very short, very tall, long hair, big nose, beautiful eyes, lots of jewelry? Exaggerate this feature. Have fun with this! You will remember the name.

Mnemonics

This word (knew-mon-icks) means a strategy to trick your mind. It allows you to play games. Let's look at three examples.

STRATEGY #87

Acronyms. Most students have used these. An acronym is a word formed from the letters (usually the first letters) of other words. Do you want to remember the names of the Great Lakes? Just remember H.O.M.E.S. This stands for Huron, Ontario, Michigan, Erie, and Superior.

STRATEGY #88

Acrostics. An acrostic uses the first letter of each word to create a sequential message. Having trouble with the order of mathematical operations? Simple. P.E.M.D.A.S. (Please Excuse My Dear Aunt Sally). Now you will forever remember to do the operation in parentheses first, followed by exponents, multiplication, division, addition, and subtraction.

Want to remember the notes assigned to the lines of a musical staff? E.G.B.D.F. (Every Good Boy Does Fine).

How about the taxonomic levels in biology? King Philip Came Over For Green Stamps (Kingdom, Phylum, Class, Order, Family, Genus, Specie).

STRATEGY #89

The hook, number, or peg system.[39] Associate a number or objects with a concept you wish to remember. Create a vivid and outrageous picture of the peg and the concept. The more vivid the image, the more of your brain is engaged, and the better chance to retain and retrieve. For instance, one memory technique can use the following number-rhyme list for a peg system:

1: gun
2: goo
3: knee
4: roar
5: hive
6: pick
7: heaven
8: bait
9: line
10: pen

Let's now assume you need to remember this list of chores:

1. clean your room
2. wash the dishes

3. feed the cats
4. write a thank-you note to your uncle
5. mow the lawn
6. set the table for dinner
7. take out the trash
8. do your homework
9. walk the dog
10. vacuum the rug

Your next task is to associate each chore with the hook number/image. Create a picture that is crystal clear and vivid. Your associations between the peg list and the items you want to remember could look like this:

1. A <u>gun</u> was held to my head until I <u>cleaned my room.</u>
2. I scrubbed and scoured all of the <u>goo</u> as <u>I washed the dishes.</u>
3. My bouncing <u>knee</u> seemed to be a comfortable place for the <u>cats to feed.</u>
4. I can just hear Uncle Bubba <u>roar</u> with laughter as he reads my <u>thank-you note.</u>
5. Bees swarmed from the <u>hive</u> when I unknowingly ran over it <u>while mowing the lawn.</u>
6. Imagine the job it was to <u>pick</u> each dish I shattered while <u>setting the table for dinner.</u>
7. <u>Heaven</u> is never having to <u>take out the trash.</u>
8. My instructors always <u>bait</u> me with an incentive to <u>complete my homework.</u>
9. Staying in a straight <u>line</u> is very difficult when <u>walking my dog.</u>
10. I finally found my <u>pen</u> when I <u>vacuumed the rug.</u>

The associations do not have to be logical. All you are trying to do is create a picture of the item you need to remember. This system can work with lists, such as vocabulary words, bones of the body, parts of speech and the like. (A word of caution though. You may remember the list, but that does not mean you understand the information. As with all the strategies in this book, pick the one that fits the situation you are facing.)

Linking. Your American government instructor just told you to know the Bill of Rights (the first ten amendments to the Constitution) by tomorrow. How will you accomplish this task? One way is to establish a story with the main points of each amendment. The more odd the picture/image/story, the better the chance of remembering it. Here's one example:

STRATEGY #90

> You can imagine the <u>expression</u> on my face when I saw the <u>armed</u> bear marching <u>troops into my house.</u> He wanted them to <u>search</u> the bathroom to make sure no one was there who might steal my <u>life, liberty, or property.</u> Just then a <u>lawyer</u> ran into the house saying the troops must be given a <u>trial by a jury</u> of bears. The tooth fairy wanted to sentence the troops to dance with wolves but this was too <u>cruel and unusual a punishment.</u> The troops were glad to be in America where they had lots of rights—<u>some written and some not.</u> The bear went to the Holiday Inn where he had a <u>reservation</u> for the night.

(The <u>underlined</u> phrases correspond to the amendments.)

Sure it's silly—but it just might be what sparks your memory. The key with linking is to establish a vivid mental picture of *relationships.* It might also make studying a bit more enjoyable. See what your imagination can do!

Practice

STRATEGY
#91

When trying to learn new material, you need to practice, practice, and practice some more. It may not be fun, but then neither are poor grades. To learn a new skill you need to perform activities that stretch your mind. Just as an athlete does stretches, calisthenics, and wind sprints to get in shape, so too you need to do mental gymnastics. I recommend Kevin Trudeau's *Mega Memory* audiotape presentation. A good portion of his approach is to use warm-up exercises designed to stretch your mind and memory. As Trudeau points out, sit-ups are used as a conditioning tool for a baseball player; but you would not expect him to do fifty in the middle of a game. This does not make them any less valuable. It's the same with mind exercises. Use them, and you will expand your capabilities.

A QUICK REVIEW

There are three steps to remembering information: noticing, storing, and retrieving.[40] You must see something, put it someplace, and then go find it.

Use hooks and linkages.

There is a difference between memory and understanding. Memory allows for the retention and retrieval of material. Understanding takes you to a higher level. The key to comprehension is the creation of relationships. You must concentrate on the task at hand. No desire, no results. You must focus your energies on the

- reasons you forget—and find a solution
- ability to identify the important information (the 80/20 principle)
- development of an efficient and effective filing system
- skill of active listening
- use of organizing models (DRC, mnemonics, mental imaging)

---

*Whatever you learn, use the new knowledge
as soon, and as often, as possible!*

Some correlations with your learning style

TOPIC	AUDITORY	KINESTHETIC	VISUAL
Storage and retrieval	acronyms and acrostics; listen to tapes; actively listen and participate in class discussions; offer alternative explanations	construct a DRC; mental imaging of movement; watch a video; use flash cards	mental imaging; flash cards; use a DRC; acronyms and acrostics
Building vocabulary	crossword puzzles	Scrabble	Pictionary

General comments about your learning environment:

- Seat location in the classroom is critical; avoid putting yourself in a distracting place.
- Limit intake of distracting stimuli.

CHAPTER 8

THERE'S NO BUSINESS LIKE PREP BUSINESS— THE ART OF BEING READY WHEN DUTY CALLS

- Introduction
- Goals
- Time management
- Classroom expectations
- Reading strategies
- Writing and research strategies
- Memory and relationships
- ✔ **Test preparation**
- Summary

1. **Bringing it all together**
   Test anxiety
   Test anxiety or inefficient test-taking strategies?
   Test preparation is not a one-time event
   Test preparation: Putting your study skills to work for you
   Competence + confidence = improved self-esteem
2. **The final checklist**
   Successful students have a plan
   Post-exam analysis
   Isn't this where we started?
   Emergency studying (a.k.a. cramming)
   Test-taking strategies: Some general suggestions
3. **A quick review**

*Every human mind is a great slumbering
power until awakened by a keen desire
and by definite resolution to do.*

—Edgar F. Roberts

BRINGING IT ALL TOGETHER

The preceding pages have presented an abundance of strategies. You may still have one question, though: "How does all this help my GPA?" Fair question. Although grades are not the be-all and end-all of your school existence, they are obviously important in our educational system.

The key point here is the importance of developing understanding and relationships. Do this, and the grades *will* follow. Perhaps you remember the saying, "Give a man a fish and you feed him for a meal. Teach him to fish and you feed him for a lifetime." These strategies are *self-generating*—not self-terminating. Learn and apply them, and you will benefit for the rest of your life.

Let's tie all of this information together.

Test Anxiety

Test: A series of questions to determine one's knowledge.

Anxiety: Distress, apprehension, worry

Test anxiety: The apprehension about one's ability to perform acceptably on a series of questions designed to determine one's knowledge.

Why do students fear exams? After all, a test is only a piece of paper with words on it. This piece of paper cannot do harm to the student. But the anxiety remains.

ACTIVITY

WHY ARE YOU ANXIOUS ABOUT EXAMS?

Circle any of the following that may cause, or have caused, you some anxious moments on test day.

- the instructor will be upset with a poor performance
- I'll be upset with a poor performance
- my parents will be upset with a poor performance
- I'll feel like a dummy if I don't do well
- a poor test grade will kill my GPA
- I mentally freeze on test day
- tests are really dumb anyway

- I know the material, but I freeze when I'm timed
- my mind drifts during the exam
- I tend to look at two or three test items at one time
- I know I could have done better if I'd crammed the night before
- I speak to myself with a lot of negative self-talk (distortions)
- I have so much nervous energy I cannot focus
- I don't have confidence in myself
- I always seem to score worse than I expect
- I fear what this exam will do to future opportunities (e.g., jobs)
- other people distract me with their movements
- I feel nauseated
- I feel tense from head to toe
- I become anxious talking at the last minute about the exam
- other reasons: _____

_____

_____

_____

Now, look at the items you circled. Do you notice any similarities between items? Closer inspection reveals the following categories:

(Y) • how you view *yourself*

(O) • how *others* perceive you

(U) • *unrealistic* goals (is your "sky" too high?)

(T) • *thought* distractions

(U) • for all your talk, you were just *unprepared*

Y.O.U T.U. (YOU TOO) can conquer test anxiety.

While the paper cannot harm you, your perception of the situation can lead you to uneasiness. It is a matter of attitude. If you lack confidence going into the exam, your perception will become reality.

Let's look at some student-tested strategies.

If you are panicky prior to exams, try this activity.   **STRATEGY**
#92

Ask yourself, "What is the worst case scenario? What is the very worst thing that can happen to me as a result of this exam?" Write your answers on a piece of paper. Now objectively evaluate what you have written. Are there any distortions in your perceptions? That is, if you look at the situation realistically, what will *probably* happen? Once you have identified this, *visualize success*. What would you tell a friend who was nervous about an exam? I doubt you would say he/she was stupid and was destined to fail. Give yourself credit for what you know and what you can do.

❖❖❖

STRATEGY #93   Try "blocking" your test paper. If your eyes tend to drift from one item to another during the exam this technique will help you focus. You'll need two blank pieces of paper. Place one piece over the item above the one you are working on and the other paper on the following one. For example, if you are working on problem 3, "block out" 2 and 4. You force your eyes to focus on only one item. (Always get your instructor's permission before using any additional pieces of paper during an exam.)

STRATEGY #94   Talk yourself through the exam. If you can sit away from other students, it might be helpful to say the test items quietly aloud. Some of my students who have used this method believe it helps them calm down to "hear" the test.

STRATEGY #95   Remove yourself from distraction. Sit as far away from any distractions as possible. Get away from windows, open doors, noisy students, and the like.

STRATEGY #96   Become familiar with format. Ask the instructor if he/she has previous exam versions to review. By becoming familiar with the teacher's particular format, you are also mastering the content.

Get a tutor. If you have been diligent with the content and assignments but still have difficulties with the subject matter, you may wish to seek additional help from the instructor or a student-tutor. The school dean or academic advisor should have information on peer tutors.

Know your material. Don't short-change yourself. The more comfortable you are with the content, the more confident you will be on the exam. Follow the strategies in this book, and there will be no reason to cram. Timely and organized studying will help you become comfortable, confident, and successful.

Are "props" allowed? If you have a math test requiring a lot of formulas, can you write each formula on an index card and use them during the exam? How about your notes? Will the instructor allow their use during the exam? (If so, it will help if you followed the strategies in Chapter 4.)

Work with a timed situation. Prior to exam day, practice the test. Do a specified number of items in a time frame that is roughly analogous to an exam situation. If you can get an old exam, complete it in the same amount of time you will have during the exam period. Become familiar and comfortable with the element of time.

STRATEGY #97

Check for alternative testing environments. If distractions are a severe problem, perhaps the instructor will allow you to complete the exam in an empty room if one is available.

Test anxiety or inefficient test-taking strategies?

Some students are not anxious about exams. They are prepared and comfortable on test day. But still they perform at a sub-par level. The problem, in this case, is one of time—they almost always run out of it. If this is your problem, try the following suggestions.

Before you start the exam, review all items. Get a feel for the test. How long will you need to do page 1? Page 2? In other words, establish a pace for yourself.

STRATEGY #98

Do the easy items first. If you do run out of time, you don't want to miss out on the free points. "Easy" refers to content as well as item type. Obviously, make sure you answer all the questions you *know*. Likewise, you may wish to breeze through the item types you are most comfortable with before you tackle the more challenging ones. If matching is easy for you, do it first.

STRATEGY #99

Underline, circle, and box key words. Don't get an item wrong because you failed to see a trigger word.

Wear a watch. It is your responsibility to keep track of time.

Prepare for content as well as the timed situation. Do as many practice tests as you can in a test-like environment. Depending on how large a concern this is for you, you may give thought to doing a practice test in the classroom for a specified period of time.

Test preparation is not a one-time event

This book has emphasized the need to relate information. You have strategies on six study skills topics. Let's examine how they are related—and how they connect to test preparation. (We will be talking about test preparation for classroom and teacher-made exams. Test preparation for exams such as the PSAT, SAT, ACT, or GRE involve other strategies that will not be addressed here.)

So where do we start getting ready for the exam? How do you prepare for an exam? When? What material do you use?

Let's examine the following model.

STRATEGY
#100

Test preparation: Putting your study skills to work for you

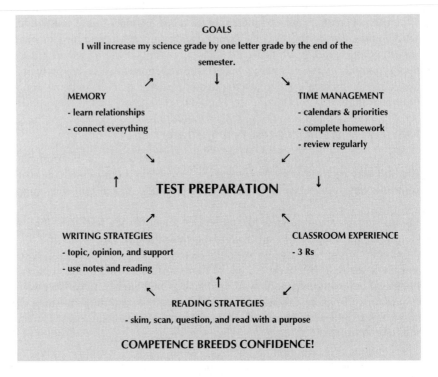

GOALS

I will increase my science grade by one letter grade by the end of the semester.

MEMORY
- learn relationships
- connect everything

TIME MANAGEMENT
- calendars & priorities
- complete homework
- review regularly

TEST PREPARATION

WRITING STRATEGIES
- topic, opinion, and support
- use notes and reading

CLASSROOM EXPERIENCE
- 3 Rs

READING STRATEGIES
- skim, scan, question, and read with a purpose

COMPETENCE BREEDS CONFIDENCE!

A review of each of the above steps looks like this:

Goals. Establish an attitude and know where you are going.

Time management. Establish your plan of how to get where you are going.

Classroom experience. Actively listen, review, reorganize, and relate.

Reading strategies. Actively read with a purpose. Relate to the big picture of the classroom experience.

Writing Strategies. Do you know enough about the topic to state an opinion and support it?

Memory. Obviously, if you can't retrieve the information, it will be extremely difficult to perform well on an exam.

Competence + confidence = improved self-esteem

TIP! If you have been diligent with the foregoing study skill strategies, one consequence is evident: Each step along the way prepares for the exam. The arrows in the preceding diagram indicate the continuous and flowing nature of these strategies. Once you understand and accept this fact, you are well on your way to becoming the successful student you have always wanted to be. No more cramming. Say goodbye to test anxiety. Welcome competence, confidence, and improved self-esteem.

This does not, however, mean that you do not need to take care of some specific test-preparation tasks immediately prior to the exam. You must consciously tie all of the material together so you can see the big picture.

Test preparation is not a one-time event. It is a process.

THE FINAL CHECKLIST

TIP! When it comes to test-taking, do not be your own worst enemy. A positive mental attitude will carry you a long way. Sometimes it is a matter of semantics. I have had teachers tell me that their students go to pieces at the mention of a "test." But tell the students they are having a "quiz," an "exercise," a "worksheet," or an "opportunity," and the anxiety is relieved immediately. If that works for you, then use it. The point here is not to get caught up in words. *Visualize* success—and then *achieve* it!

A certain amount of anxiety may even be useful. It can provide just the right edge to keep you on your toes during the test. Likewise, confidence is fine—but arrogance can be devastating. Your assessment of your abilities and preparation must bear some resemblance to reality.

Successful students have a plan

Tests are opportunities for you to shine and show your stuff! Many students, unfortunately, think studying for a test means looking at their notes the night before the exam. Effective test preparation requires continual review and practice.

As the big day approaches, successful students establish a plan. Use the following tool to get organized, reduce your levels of anxiety—and do well on your latest opportunity.

TEST-PREPARATION CHECKLIST (✓)

Class: _____ Instructor: _____ Test date and time:_____

Type of exam:
❏ multiple choice
❏ true/false
❏ matching
❏ completion
❏ identification
❏ essay
❏ lab work
❏ problems
❏ other _____

What do I need when I study:
❏ textbook
❏ notes
❏ teacher's study guide
❏ worksheets
❏ past exams (can be very helpful)
❏ supplemental readings
❏ calculator
❏ pens, pencils, paper
❏ other _____

Will I study alone or with a study group?   ❏ alone   ❏ study groups*
[*A word of caution about study groups: Make sure they are more study than social. Set an agenda.]

Are there any study sessions the teacher will lead before or after class?   ❏ yes   ❏ no

If "yes," when?_____

When will I study? Make a plan—and stick to it!

Date/time:_____

Date/time:_____

Date/time:_____
 Put these dates on your calendar.

Prioritization. What topics will the exam cover?

Topic	I really know this stuff	I am not too sure about this stuff	I have no clue about this stuff!	Topic reviewed at least once
1.				
2.				
3.				
4.				

Predict some test questions. (This forces you to focus on key concepts the teacher has been stressing.)

What I need for test day: ❑ pens, pencils, paper (lined, unlined, graph)
❑ calculator
❑ notes—can I use my notes during the test?
❑ textbook—is the test open-book?
❑ ruler
❑ wristwatch
❑ tissue for sniffles
❑ other _____

Test preparation does not end when you hand in your test. Start preparing for your next exam by doing a post-exam analysis.

I was most prepared for _____

I was not well prepared for _____

    Why?_____

What helped me the most: ❑ my notes
❑ my homework
❑ tutoring sessions
❑ my study schedule
❑ my study group
❑ my study environment
❑ other _____

My major weakness(es):   ❑ ran out of time during the test
❑ did not expect this type of exam
❑ studied the wrong material
❑ did not start studying early enough

Grade I *realistically* expect to receive _____   Grade I received _____

My r*ealistic* plan to improve for the next exam is _____

_____

_____

_____

A common reaction by many students following the completion of an exam is to forget it and concentrate on the next opportunity. Although this is an understandable reaction, the successful student needs to pause, even if momentarily, and reflect on the exam.

Post-exam analysis

Look at the above checklist once again. Notice that the last portion is a post-exam analysis. This type of activity accomplishes a couple of things. While the material is still fresh in your mind, content review is critical. There is a good chance you will see some of this information again. Make sure you have it correct now. Don't get it wrong on two consecutive exams. From a process point of view, it is important to understand what worked and what did not work for you. The successful student wishes to improve. There is no need for obsessive-compulsive behavior; but why not identify your challenges and strengths?

Isn't this where we started?

STRATEGY #102 Look back at Chapter 2. The first activity was an assessment of your strengths and weaknesses. Are you seeing a pattern here?

All these strategies are a continual process. By reviewing, reorganizing, and relating (the 3 Rs), you are able to move forward. The post-exam analysis places you back at the goal-setting stage. Now you are ready to improve your performance, establish a goal, then evaluate, and improve again.

That's really all there is to it.

Emergency studying (a.k.a. cramming)[41]

But what do you do if you have *not* kept up? How do you survive a test when you're down to the night before, and you aren't ready? Here are some pointers for emergency studying. Please remember this is not desirable—but if it's all you have, then let's get the most from it.

Do Not. . .

- Be tempted to read everything quickly you haven't read yet. If you read large quantities of material too fast, you will have poor recall. Why waste your time?
- Panic! O.K., so you did not study as you wish you had. Test day is no time to panic.
- Give up. Especially on essay exams—never leave the item blank. Think! You surely can come up with something to write. You just may get credit.

Do. . .

- Accept the fact that you will not be able to study everything.
- Relax. Take a deep breath.
- Start by anticipating your teacher: What type of questions will the teacher ask? What types of content and/or skills will be tested? Recall? Relationships? (This will be much easier if you have been practicing the 3 Rs. See Chapter 4.)
- Go to your notes and text to find the most important material. Clues to guide you: chapter titles and sub-titles, major emphasis in class discussions and lectures, relationships with past material, chapter summaries. (Refer to the reading plan in Chapter 5.)
- The following when you find important information:

  read it

  ask yourself a question for which the information is an answer say the information to yourself

check to see if you were correct

repeat the process

- Try to find and study some important information from every chapter that was assigned.
- *__Next time study in advance!__*

Test-taking: *Some general suggestions*

- Get a good night's sleep prior to the exam. Do not study right up until your bedtime. Give your brain a rest and do something non-academic before going to bed. Otherwise, you might wake up feeling as if you have not had a break. You want to be a sharp as possible going into the test.
- Depending on the time of the exam, eat a good meal for breakfast/lunch—but too much food might leave you groggy. An exception: If you don't eat breakfast or lunch, and that works for you, then ignore this suggestion. Use strategies that fit your lifestyle and personality. My bias, confirmed by most research, is to urge a well-balanced nutritional meal.
- Have all your tools with you (see the Test-Preparation Checklist).
- Wear a watch, or at the very least, have the class clock in sight. Keep track of time—this is your responsibility, not the teacher's. But remember, those school-issued room clocks are notorious for being slow, fast, or broken.
- Read *all* instructions carefully. Do not start until you know what you are expected to do. There is not a prize for finishing first.
- More than likely, the wording on the exam will be different than what you found in your book, or what the teacher said in class. That is why it is important to *know* your material. Do not just memorize. Relate to the big picture. Review the strategies in Chapter 7.

Multiple-choice tests:

read carefully. Look for words like *not, except, which is incorrect, best, all, always, never, none*

cover all the answer choices before you look at them. Treat the item like a fill-in-the-blank question. Come up with an answer before you look at the choices. This might help you from being swayed by a "trick" answer

if you are not sure of an answer, use the process-of-elimination strategy to arrive at the correct answer. At least you can narrow your options and make an educated guess

answer the easy questions first. Save the tough ones for the end.

underline key words

if you are using an answer sheet, make sure you transfer your answers to the correct number on the answer sheet

STRATEGY #103

STRATEGY #104

Matching tests:

    read all the answer choices first

    cross out the items you pick

    are you allowed to use an answer more than once?

    answer the easy items first. Save the tough ones for the end.

STRATEGY #105

Essay tests (Review Chapter 6):

    Know what your task is. Once again, know these key words:

      analyze: to divide a topic or issue into its parts; show the relation of one part to another

      apply: use your knowledge in a new or different situation

      assess: to judge the merits of some issue; evaluate

      classify: to put things into categories

      compare: to provide similarities, differences, consequences (see *analyze* above)

      contrast: to provide differences

      criticize: to judge critically

      defend: to argue for a particular issue

      describe: to explain an event, issue, topic; what are main characteristics

      discuss: to explain in detail; go beyond mere description

      evaluate: to judge, criticize, establish standards

      identify: to show how something is unique or individual

      illustrate: to provide examples

      interpret: to describe the meaning of an issue

      motivations: what caused something to happen

      relative importance: to show how two or more factors compare to one another

      summarize: to restate briefly

      trace: to provide an order or sequence of events

    Know what the topic is.

    Develop a main idea and follow this.

    Support your thesis with substantial facts; don't insult the teacher with "fluff."

    Pay attention to grammar and sentence structure.

    Never leave an essay item blank. Put something down—you just might get credit! Don't forget to use the clustering strategy.

    If you tend to get writer's block, practice the strategies introduced in Chapter 6.

As you prepare for the exam, be kind to yourself. Don't sit there saying you are going to fail. Establish a goal and go for it! If you want to be a successful student, you need to carry a positive attitude in your book bag.

A QUICK REVIEW

Effective test preparation starts at the completion of the most recent exam. This does not mean continual round-the-clock studying. In fact, follow the methods in this book, and your study time should be drastically cut.

But for this to become a reality, you must:

- see the seven topics as part of an interconnected whole, not as distinct entities
- know if, and why, you are anxious about exams
- be an efficient test taker
- be familiar with your instructors' testing styles
- start preparing for the next exam right after completing the most recent exam
- always take a moment to do a post-exam analysis

Focus on success—Not excuses.

Some correlations with your learning style

TOPIC	AUDITORY	KINESTHETIC	VISUAL
Preparing for the exam	3 Rs; tape record potential exam questions	write questions on flash cards	write potential exam questions
During the exam	preview entire exam; methodically work through items simplest to more difficult; if appropriate (and not distracting to others) say items aloud	preview entire exam; physically block out all but the item you are working on	preview entire exam; mark up exam as much as helpful

General comments about your learning environment:

- Is a study group appropriate for you?
- Set up a schedule of studying to coincide with your "peak times."
- Limit distracting stimuli.
- Nutritional habits and sleep habits should be conducive to successful test performance.

CHAPTER 9

SOME FINAL COMMENTS

- Introduction
- Goals
- Time management
- Classroom expectations
- Reading strategies
- Writing and research strategies
- Memory and relationships
- Test preparation
- ✔ Summary

You will become as small as your controlling desire; as great as your dominant aspiration.

—*James Allen*

THE P.O.P R.A.P. LIST[42]

The literature on study and organizational skills comes down to a few major principles. Each author and instructor has a different angle, but the bottom line is the same. If you take nothing else from this book, remember these basic tenets.

1. **You need to know your <u>P</u>urpose and mission as a student.** You have to make the commitment to focus on success and be a successful student.
2. **In order to be that successful student—that is, the best that you can be— you must <u>O</u>rganize your time.** You cannot control others, but you can surely control your own actions.
3. **Don't hinder yourself with defeatist attitudes. Be <u>P</u>ositive.** Visualize success and aim for it. Be realistic but also challenge yourself.
4. **<u>R</u>eview, reorganize, and relate.** There is a difference between memorizing and understanding.
5. **Be an <u>A</u>ctive learner.** Know where your instructors are going with a lesson. Follow them—maybe get there ahead of them. But don't just sit there.
6. **Finally, look at all of these strategies and <u>P</u>ick, mix, and match to suit your personality and temperament.** If you learn these strategies, adapt them to your learning style, practice them faithfully, and apply them to your studies, you will see improvement. Studying is a process.

I wish you continued success as you engage the wonderful world of learning.

APPENDIXES

APPENDIX A

Narrowing Your Research Topic

Here is an actual student example. A student of mine was assigned a ten-page research paper for a United States history class. The topic was very general: Pick any topic in post-1865 American history and develop a research paper.

Talk about broad! Although students may dislike rigid guidelines, there is something to be said for the structure such requirements provide. This assignment was challenging due to the vast array of topics the student could choose.

After some initial discussion, he decided to focus on the late nineteenth century. Now what? Where would you go to get your initial topic? What would you use to jump-start your writing battery?

This student decided to use what he had on hand—his class textbook. He reviewed the table of contents, chapter headings, and time lines. He was searching for any broad themes he could pursue. This was a start, but he was still not sure what to do. So he decided to brainstorm on paper.

Across the top of a piece of notebook paper he wrote the following broad areas: Politics, Economics, Social, and Culture. From here, with the help of class notes and the text, and in no particular order, he listed historical concepts and events. Keep in mind, all the student wanted to do at this stage was to get something on paper—write now, pick and choose later. Here is what his listing looked like:

POLITICS	ECONOMICS	SOCIAL	CULTURE
-elections	-distribution of wealth	-class develop.	-high cult.
-1896	-rise of corporation	-immigrants	-low cult.
-military and mobilizing for war	-robber barons or captains of industry	-good -bad	-parks -b-ball -saloons
-suffrage	-labor unions		-pub. school
-isolation v. globalism	-gilded age		
-Monroe Doctrine	-Alger and the Amer. Dream		
-reform and scandals			

Now the student had something with which to work. His next step was to pick one of the above. After doing some cursory reading, he settled on a topic: immigrants.

What do you think the next step was? What would you do?

He still had to narrow the focus. *What* about immigrants would he research? He came up with several choices:

New immigrants v. old immigrants: Why did the nations of origin start to change?

Discrimination: What form(s) did discrimination take? Why did it exist? Was it more perceived than reality?

Occupations: What industries attracted specific immigrant groups? Why?

Residential patterns: Where did the immigrants live? Why? Did they mingle with other immigrant groups? Why or why not?

Eventually, the student decided to tackle the topic of occupations. He had a guiding question for his research.

Remember to be flexible as you do your research. You may need to make an adjustment, based on your research, and move in a *slightly* different direction than you originally thought.

The key: Do enough initial research so that you can make an intelligent decision on which topic and question to focus. If you don't, you will end up wasting time and creating undue stress for yourself.

APPENDIX B

Reading Strategies: Establishing purpose in a reading assignment

Here are some questions you may have developed for the activity starting on page 75 in Chapter 5.

INTRODUCTION

Fundamental concepts of biology	Possible questions: What are the fundamental concepts of biology? What is biology? What does biology study? What questions does biology answer?
Evolution and natural selection	Possible questions: What is evolution? What is natural selection? Are they connected? What questions do both of these theories attempt to answer? I've heard that evolution is controversial. Why? Who or what is naturally selected?
Adaptations	Possible questions: Adaptations of what or whom? Why do adaptations occur? How do they occur? Is this part of evolution?
Energy and natural selection	Possible questions: What is the connection between energy and natural selection? From where does the energy come? Is there a relationship with adaptations?

Scientific method	Possible questions: What is the scientific method? Do all scientists use it? Do only scientists use it? How is it used? Why is it used?
Observations and hypotheses	Possible questions: How are observations done? Who does them? What is an hypothesis? Do hypotheses always come from observations?
Experiments	Possible questions: What are the elements of an experiment? Have I ever conducted an experiment? If so, what was it that I actually did? Is an experiment different from an observation? Why would I do an experiment rather than an observation?
Limitations of experiments	Possible questions: What are the limitations of experiments? Why are they considered limitations? Can these limitations be avoided? If there are limitations, why do people still do experiments?
Correlation studies	Possible questions: What is a correlation? Why are correlation studies conducted? How are the results used?
It's a fact?	Possible questions: What is a fact? How is the concept of "fact" related to the discipline of biology? Can I question a fact?
Humans and environment	Possible questions: What is the relationship between humans and the environment? What does this relationship have to do with the study of biology?
Summary	Possible questions: Can I summarize what I just read? What are the main points? Can I write a brief conclusion about all this material? Can I participate intelligently in a class discussion on this chapter? What were the most troubling concepts? What questions do I need to ask my instructor?

APPENDIX C

Developing a Data Retrieval Chart

(Developed from the reading passage activity starting on page 126 in Chapter 7.) Compare your data retrieval chart to the one below. Keep in mind that this chart can, and probably will, differ from yours. The point is to plot the relationships you see. This chart will not only help you place information into a retrievable location in your memory, it is also a great way to take reading notes (Chapter 5) and study for an exam (Chapter 8).

THEORY	BACKGROUND	CONCEPTS	SUMMARY	EVALUATION
Conflict	Marx: opposing classes	change; modern class diversity; purpose of classes; economics is critical	class conflict is major impetus for social change	[what is your personal reaction to this theory; anticipate an essay question]
Functionalist	Parsons	unequal distribution of rewards; motivation; fair v. excessive	classes are necessary for society to advance and progress	[what is your personal reaction to this theory; anticipate an essay question]
Interactionist	conflict and functionalists don't explain intra-class distinctions	prestige; status; "symbols of membership"	group behaviors emphasize intra-class divisions	[what is your personal reaction to this theory; anticipate an essay question]

APPENDIX D

Checklist of selected tips and strategies

ACTIVITY

As a last review, write a brief description of how each of the following will help you become a more successful student:

GOALS

Identification of learning styles

Connection between strengths and challenges

Desire

Responsibility

Attitude

Active learning

Practice

Connection between competence and confidence

Break time

Incentives

Developing keen insight

Establish a plan

Goals: written, specific, and realistic

Anticipation of glitches

W.I.N.

Balance: academic life and non-academic life

Periodic goal evaluation and adjustment

The buddy system

TIME MANAGEMENT

Flexibility

The 168 hour week

Identifying problem areas

Identifying causes of problems

Note-taking: Traditional outline

Note-taking: Cluster notes

Note-taking: Two-in-one notes

Note-taking: "Scatter" notes

Note-taking: Be consistent

Ongoing study guides

3 Rs

T/S/3 Cs

Importance of a notebook

READING STRATEGIES

Establishing a purpose

Different books = different approaches

Focusing on ideas

Warming up

Skimming

Scanning

Establishing questions

Establish tasks

Notes on reading

Outline to class

Using supplemental sources

Vocabulary building

Charactergrams

WRITING STRATEGIES

Purpose?

Read instructions aloud

Analyze the prompt

Make basic decisions

Planning a response

Look at your T.O.E.S.

The 5 & 5 principle

Keep it to the point

Clustering

Jump-starting your writing battery

Why is the topic/opinion important?

Key words—know the vocabulary

Make a plan

Post-writing assessment

Organizing for a research paper

Narrowing a topic

Electronic catalogs

MEMORY AND RELATIONSHIPS

Recognize *why* you forget

Learn how to forget!

Label your filing cabinet

Use it or lose it

Memory $\neq$ understanding

Frustration is OK

Active listening: Focus on the speaker

Active listening: Find relevance

Active listening: Listen, don't speak

Active listening: Participate

Active listening: Ask questions

Active listening: Apply the knowledge

Connect homework with class work

The data retrieval chart

Think in pictures

Names—find a link

Acronyms

Acrostics

Hooks

Use new knowledge as soon as possible

TEST PREPARATION

This is the pay-off topic

Test anxiety: Recognizing and solving

Be kind to yourself

Test-taking efficiency

Visualize success

Confidence without arrogance

The checklist

Post-exam analysis—establish a modified goal

Emergency studying

Get sleep

Get food

Do you have your tools?

Wearing your watch?

Carefully read instructions

Key words

SUMMARY

The P.O.P. R.A.P. list

Continue to read, write, and learn!

ENDNOTES

[1]A great deal has been written about learning styles. My intent here is to provide a brief overview. Matte and Henderson, *Success Your Style!: Right- & Left-Brain Techniques for Learning* 1995; Dunn and Dunn, *Teaching Students Through Their Individual Learning Styles: A Practical Approach,* 1978; and Swartz, *Accelerated Learning: How You Learn Determines What You Learn,* 1991, may be of interest to those wishing to do further reading. Also see, Keefe, *Learning Style Handbook: II. Accommodating Perceptual, Study and Instructional Preferences,* 1989; and Lazear, *Seven Ways of Knowing: Teaching for Multiple Intelligences,* 1991.

[2]Thomas Armstrong, *Multiple Intelligences in the Classroom.* (Alexandria, Virginia: Association for Supervision and Curriculum Development, 1994), 2. Armstrong, in a very straightforward manner, describes and analyzes the seven intelligences identified by Howard Gardner. They are: linguistic intelligence, logical-mathematical intelligence, spatial intelligence, bodily-kinesthetic, musical intelligence, interpersonal intelligence, and intrapersonal intelligence.

[3]Rita Dunn and Kenneth Dunn, *Teaching Students Through Their Individual Styles: A Practical Approach* (Reston, VA, Reston Publishing Company, Inc. 1978), 4; 402-404.

[4]Please note that I am not addressing specific learning disabilities in this book.

[5]Claude W. Olney, *Where There's a Will There's an "A"* (Paoli, Pennsylvania: Chesterbrook Educational Publishers, Inc., 1990), videocassette.

[6]Henry E. Florey, *Study Orientation Skills: Participant Manual* (Tuscaloosa, Alabama: Author, 1978), 21.

[7]Also, see Roger C. Swartz, *Accelerated Learning: How you learn determines what you learn* (Durant, Oklahoma: EMIS, 1991), 61. Mr. Swartz states, "A decline in recall occurs, especially for material studied during the mid-point of the process, if study periods are too lengthy."

[8]Zig Ziglar, *How to Get What You Want* (New York: Simon and Schuster, 1978), audiocassette.

[9]For a more detailed discussion, refer to Susan B. Wilson, *Goal Setting* (New York: American Management Association, 1994), 4-9.

[10]Elizabeth Winstead, "Mastering Time Management" (Jacksonville, Florida: Jacksonville University, no date), presentation.

[11]Sarah Gilbert, *Go for It: Get Organized* (New York: Morrow Jr. Books, 1990).

[12]Ron Fry, *How to Study* (Hawthorne, New Jersey: The Career Press, 1991), 84.

[13]Adam Robinson, *What Smart Students Know: Maximum Grades. Optimum Learning. Minimum Time* (New York: HarperPerennial, 1990), 81-82.

[14]Covey, *The 7 Habits of Highly Effective People,* audiocassette; Stephen Covey et.al., *First Things First.* New York: Simon and Schuster, 1994.

[15]For an excellent presentation on this dichotomy, I recommend Stephen Covey, *First Things First,* p. 26.

[16]As with most teachers, I have learned so much from my students. This pearl of wisdom comes by way of a former high school student and still close friend, Terry Kaden.

[17]Also see Dave Ellis, *Becoming a Master Student,* 7th ed. (Boston, Massachusetts: Houghton Mifflin, 1994), 139; and Walter Pauk, *How to Study in College,* 5th ed. (Boston, Massachusetts: Houghton Mifflin, 1993), 65-66.

[18]This style of notes has been refered to by various labels. Some call it mapping, others like Matte and Henderson use the term "spidergram."

[19]Walter Pauk, *How to Study in College,* 110-114.

[20]For a more in-depth presentation of this method I recommend Nancy Lightfoot Matte and Susan Hilary Green Henderson, *Success Your Style!: Right- & Left-Brain Techniques for Learning* (Belmont, California: Wadsworth Publishing Company, 1995), passim.

[21]Ron Fry, *Improve Your Reading,* 18.

[22]Dave Ellis, *Becoming a Master Student,* 7th ed., 117.

[23]Adam Robinson, *What Smart Students Know,* 36-37.

[24]Spencer A. Rathus, *Psychology in the New Millennium,* 6th ed. (Fort Worth, Texas: Harcourt Brace, 1996), chapter 1.

[25]Karen Arms and Pamela S. Camp, *Biology,* 4th ed. (Fort Worth, Texas: Saunders College Publishing, 1995), chapter 1.

[26]Mortimer Adler and Charles Van Doren, *How To Read a Book* (NY: Simon and Schuster, 1972), 102.

[27]Adler and Van Doren, *How To Read a Book,* Chapters 13 to 19, passim.

[28]Louis E. Boone and David L. Kurtz, *Contemporary Business,* 8th ed. (Fort Worth: Dryden Press, 1996), 122-130.

[29]So many writers and teachers have used this method that I cannot attribute it to one particular individual. For a particularly detailed explanation I refer the reader to Sheila Bender, *Writing Personal Essays: How to Shape Your Life Experiences for the Page* (Cincinnati, Ohio: Writers Digest Books, 1995), passim.

[30]David Marshak, *Learning a Study Skills Program, Level II,* 3rd ed. (Reston, VA: National Association of Secondary School Principals, 1995). The NAASP has developed an excellent series of study skills programs for primary and secondary grade levels.

[31]For a clear and simple organizing tool I recommend Michael Edmondson, "The History Paper, Part III," in *OAH Magazine of History,* Fall 1995, 31-35.

[32]One such resource is Jean Key Gates, *Guide to the Use of Libraries and Information Sources,* 7th ed. (New York: McGraw-Hill, Inc., 1994.)

[33]For instance, LUIS (Library User Information System) is the electronic catalog used for the state of Florida public universities.

[34]See Appendix A for another example of how to narrow a research topic.

[35]Joan Minninger and Eleanor Dugan, *Rapid Memory in 7 Days: The Quick-and-Easy Guide to Better Remembering* (New York: The Berkeley Publishing Group, 1994), 17.

[36]Kevin Trudeau, *Mega Memory* (Illinois: Nightingale Conant Corporation, 1991), audiocassettes.

[37]William Kornblum, *Sociology in a Changing World,* 3rd ed. (Fort Worth, Texas: Harcourt Brace, 1994), 173-175.

[38]Both Trudeau and Roger Swartz praise the power of mental pictures. Swartz believes we will have more efficient retention if we associate material with images that are "... nonsensical, ridiculous, sensual, bizarre," colorful and on a grand scale. (*Accelerated Learning,* 94-95).

[39]This system is introduced in many study skills books and programs. Some use the same words, some use variations; but the principle is the same. For further discussions see Florey, *Study Orientation Skills: Participant Manual, 60:* Minninger and Dugan, *Rapid Memory in 7 Days,* 86-87; Matte and Henderson, *Success Your Style*, pp. 115-117.

[40]Minninger and Dugan, *Rapid Memory in 7 Days,* 27-41.

[41]These are basic suggestions you can find in a number of sources. I would like to specifically acknowledge *The Teachers As Advisors Manual* (Jacksonville, FL: Stanton College Preparatory School, no date.)

[42]The observant student will notice I have applied the "acronym" strategy introduced in Chapter 7.

SELECTED BIBLIOGRAPHY

[Success will be fostered by further reading and research. I have found the following sources especially helpful as I prepared this book.]

Adler, Mortimer and Charles Van Doren, *How to Read a Book.* New York: Simon and Schuster, 1972.

Armstrong, Thomas. *Multiple Intelligences in the Classroom.* Alexandria, Virginia: Association for Supervision and Curriculum Development, 1994.

Bender, Sheila. *Writing Personal Essays: How to Shape Your Life Experiences for the Page.* Cincinnati, Ohio: Writer's Digest Books, 1995.

Canter, Lee and Lee Hausner. *Homework Without Tears.* New York: HarperPerennial, 1987.

Coman, Marcia and Kathy Heavers. *How to Improve Your Study Skills.* Chicago: VGM Career Horizons/NTC Publishing Group, 1990.

Covey, Stephen R. *The 7 Habits of Highly Effective People.* New York: Simon and Schuster, 1989. Audiocassette tape.

Covey, Stephen R., A. Roger Merrill, and Rebecca R. Merrill. *First Things First.* New York: Simon and Schuster, 1994.

Disney University Professional Development Programs. *Creating Motivational Learning Environments.* Walt Disney World Company, 1995.

Ellis, Dave. *Becoming a Master Student,* 7th ed. Boston, Houghton Mifflin Company, 1994.

Florey, Henry E. Jr. *Study Orientation Skills: Participant Manual.* Tuscaloosa, Alabama: Author, 1978.

Fry, Ron. *How To Study.* Hawthorne, New Jersey: The Career Press, 1991. [This series includes various titles: *Manage Your Time, Write Papers, Take Notes, Improve Your Reading, Ace Any Test, Improve Your Memory.*]

Gilbert, Sarah. *Go for It: Get Organized.* New York: Morrow Jr. Books, 1990.

Green, Gordon W., Jr. *Helping Your Child Learn.* New York: Carol Publishing Group, 1994.

Keefe, James. *Learning Style Profile Handbook: II. Accommodating Perceptual, Study and Instructional Performances.* Reston, Virginia: National Association of Secondary School Principals.

Koepple, Mary Sue. *Writing Resources for Conferencing and Collaboration.* New Jersey: Prentice-Hall, 1989.

Lazear, David. *Seven Ways of Knowing: Teaching for Multiple Intelligences.* Palatine, Illinois: Skylight Publishing, 1991.

Margulies, Nancy. *Mapping Inner Space: Learning and Teaching Mind Mapping.* Tucson, Arizona: Zephyr Press, 1991.

Marshak, David. *Learning and Study Skills Program, Level II.* 3rd ed. Reston, Virginia: National Association of Secondary School Principals, 1995.

Matte, Nancy Lightfoot and Susan Hilary Green Henderson. *Success Your Style!: Right- and Left-Brain Techniques for Learning.* Belmont, California: The Wadsworth Publishing Company, 1995.

Minninger, Joan and Eleanor Dugan. *Rapid Memory in 7 Days: The Quick-and-Easy Guide to Better Remembering.* New York: Perigee Books, 1994.

Noble, William. *The 28 Biggest Writing Blunders: (And How to Avoid Them).* Cincinnati, Ohio: Writer's Digest Books, 1992.

Olney, Claude W. *Where There's a Will There's an "A".* Paoli, Pennsylvania: Chesterbrook Educational Publishers, Inc., 1990. Videocassette.

Pauk, Walter. *How To Study in College,* 4th ed. New York: Houghton Mifflin Company, 1989

Robinson, Adam. *What Smart Students Know: Maximum Grades. Optimum Learning. Minimum Time.* New York: Crown Trade Paperbacks, 1993.

Scharf-Hunt, Diana and Pam Hait. *Studying Smart: Time Management for College Students.* New York: HarperPerennial, 1990

Silver, Theodore. *Study Smart: Hands-on, Nuts-and-Bolts Techniques for Earning Higher Grades.* New York: Villard Books, 1992.

Swartz, Roger G. *Accelerated Learning: How You Learn Determines What You Learn.* Durant, Oklahoma: EMIS, 1991.

Trudeau, Kevin. *Mega Memory.* Illinois: Nightingale Conant Corporation, 1991. Audio-cassette tapes.

Wilson, Susan B. *Goal Setting.* New York: American Management Association, 1994.

Winstead, Elizabeth. "Mastering Time Management." Jacksonville, Florida: Jacksonville University, no date. A seminar presentation.

Ziglar, Zig. *How to Get What You Want.* New York: Simon and Schuster, 1978. Audio-cassette tape.

INDEX